cali'flour kitchen

cali'flour kitchen

125 Cauliflower-Based Recipes for the Carbs You Crave

AMY LACEY

with LEDA SCHEINTAUB

ABRAMS, NEW YORK

Editor: Holly Dolce
Designer: Deb Wood
Production Manager: Denise LaCongo

Library of Congress Control Number: 2018945585
ISBN: 978-1-4197-3596-7
eISBN: 978-1-68335-583-0

Printed and bound in the United States

10 9 8 7 6 5 4 3 2 1

Abrams books are available at special discounts when purchased in quantity for premiums and promotions as well as fundraising or educational use. Special editions can also be created to specification. For details, contact specialsales@abramsbooks.com or the address below.

ABRAMS The Art of Books
195 Broadway, New York, NY 10007
abramsbooks.com

This book is dedicated to my family, whose unconditional love carried me through sleepless nights and all the stumbling blocks of a first-time author. It is a testament to your faith in me and would not have been possible without your endless support and patience.

To my husband, Jim, my rock of twenty-four years—thank you for choosing me every day. Life has thrown a lot our way, but I can always count on your steady hand for comfort, whether you are at my bedside when I'm sick or right beside me in the kitchen testing new recipes. You have selflessly and flawlessly performed the roles of father, husband, and business partner, often without the recognition you deserve. This is but a small tribute to your contributions in helping Cali'flour Foods successfully create a new food category, keeping our home full of love and laughter, and being my biggest cheerleader.

And to my amazing kids, James, Caroline, and Grant: You are my greatest blessings in life. I know the craziness of the past few years has been hard sometimes, but I am forever grateful for your encouraging letters and late-night texts when I'm away from home. You give me the strength to keep going on my hardest days. I hope what you hold in your hands inspires you to always dream without limitations.

Cali'flour Foods founder Amy Lacey

introduction

As children, we all learned the popular saying "An apple a day keeps the doctor away." Well, after fifteen years of motherhood and raising three picky eaters, I, Amy Lacey, am here to challenge that age-old maxim with a modern twist: "A cauliflower a day keeps most sickness at bay."

Like many great romances, my love affair with this cruciferous veggie has been both tumultuous and profoundly life-changing. It all started on an unassuming Friday night in 2012. Fridays in the Lacey household followed a treasured family tradition: indulging in pizza and battling it out on board games (we're a competitive bunch!).

After many lively Friday nights without a hiccup, you can imagine my surprise waking up one Saturday morning to sausage-size fingers reminiscent of my pregnancy days. But this time my inflated hands did not bear good news. All my joints were hurting, and I felt awful. I couldn't even muster the energy to get out of bed (and not just because my energetic kids had kicked my butt at Settlers of Catan the previous evening).

Not long after, I developed a strange rash on my chest that doctors assumed was poison oak. I honestly thought nothing of it, until a routine surgery landed me in the hospital with a life-threatening pulmonary embolism. Many lab tests later, I was hit with a perfect storm of diagnoses: mixed connective tissue disorder, Sjogren's syndrome, and lupus. Stomaching the news was hard; I felt like I had been punched in the gut. To add insult to injury, our pizza nights were put on hold indefinitely until my doctors could stop my body from attacking itself.

Without warning, I had gone from Amy Lacey to a nameless statistic, one of fifty million people who suffer from an autoimmune disease in the United States. It's hard not to let your diagnosis take your identity, but it breaks you down in ways you don't expect.

I was faced with a hard choice: Either suffer the symptoms of this disease and let nature take its ugly course, or take a medication that might cause me to go blind or harm my kidneys. Neither option gave me the life I wanted or allowed me to be the mother and wife my family needed. I am stubborn to a fault and refused to accept my grim prognosis. There had to be a better way—I would make a better way.

With the help of my loving husband, Jim, who also happens to be a brilliant physician, I poured my time into extensive research and discovered that my diet was a huge contributing factor to my illness. Rather than slapping a temporary Band-Aid on my condition with my prescribed pills, I started tracking the foods I ate to see which ones triggered my symptoms. I found that gluten was the biggest culprit, with sugar ranking a close second. Like a bad boyfriend, eliminating these from my diet was a tough breakup. But my health and entire future were at stake, so I put on my big-girl pants (quite literally, because my body was swollen) and said goodbye to my first loves: gluten and sugar.

Almost like magic, my inflammation decreased virtually overnight. As I began to add more vegetables to my diet, I felt even better. Still, I missed family traditions with my husband and kids. I oh-so-badly craved a cheesy bite of pizza. And most of all, I missed feeling good and enjoying life on my own terms with the people I love.

Like many of you, I felt overwhelmed trying to balance everything. How would I find the time to cook healthier meals, battle my autoimmune disease, be fully present in my work, spend quality time with my family, and keep up with my household responsibilities? So naturally, I did as any insanely busy person would do—I hopped down the Pinterest rabbit hole to scroll my worries and fears away!

In all seriousness, I had come across several DIY cauliflower crust recipes on Pinterest that I was interested in trying out. Thus began the chronicle of cauliflower crust experiments that took over the Lacey home kitchen. We had family, friends, and a fellow health coach all helping at these early stages. After much trial and error (and a few accidents that left me covered in cauliflower from head to toe, laughing hysterically with my kids), we finally came up with a crust that (1) held together perfectly, (2) was nutrient-packed with a full serving of fresh cauliflower, and (3) surprisingly didn't taste like cauliflower! As a bonus, it could be repurposed as sandwich bread or the "noodles" in lasagna, among many other tasty things.

More impressive, the crust left me free of inflammation and passed the taste test of my three picky eaters, and our friends and extended family loved it too! Pizza night was officially back on in our house! It was a huge victory, but the battle was yet to be won.

Now that we had found the perfect, convenient solution to the DIY cauliflower crust disasters that plagued so many people's lives, I knew this yummy little secret was too good not to share with the world. With the savings from my previous business, a small loan from the bank, and a whole lot of passion and perseverance, Cali'flour Foods was launched.

My original desire with Cali'flour Foods was simply to reinvent one of my favorite foods by omitting the gluten that was causing me so much pain and inflammation. I had hoped to help a few others like me in the process, but I never expected to start an entire movement! In fact, I'll let you in on a secret: I wasn't even a fan of cauliflower until I bought some to make my first cauliflower pizza. But once a little experimenting revealed the vegetable's incredible versatility, I was hooked.

These days, of course, cauliflower reigns supreme in my house. Cauliflower pizza is a weekly staple, as are other cauliflower-based dishes, including pancakes, waffles, white sauce, and more. You know how you can't fully appreciate something until you've experienced the good and the ugly? My love for cauliflower deepened while hand-processing hundreds of pounds for production, leaving me smelling like cauliflower for days afterward. I was once even put out of commission for a week after slipping on a piece of cauliflower, skating across the entire room, and falling flat on my butt!

But my persistence in perfecting the crusts paid off. I made Cali'flour Foods a family affair, involving my husband and three kids as well as any relative or friend we could coerce into helping us. Even now, the close team we've built through the company feels just like family.

From its humble beginnings at the farmers' market in my hometown of Chico, California, Cali'flour Foods has now expanded to grocery stores across the nation and nabbed the number-one best-selling spot on Amazon for all pizza crusts. Cali'flour Foods was the first cauliflower pizza on the market, and the company has grown exponentially every year. We have become a pioneer in offering delicious low-calorie, low-carb, grain-free alternatives to traditional pizza. Our recipes allow people to enjoy "splurge" foods such as lasagna, sandwiches, and chips without compromising their health. Our crusts have generated buzz in Hollywood and beyond, and they appeal to people across the dietary spectrum with all types of health considerations, from celiac disease to diabetes, Weight Watchers to dairy-free, plus vegan, paleo, keto, and the general plant-conscious. It makes believers of the most veggie-fearing folks among us.

People are drawn to our crusts because they are simple, delicious, and so healthy that they elevate pizza to a superfood. Most gluten-free pizza crusts are filled with unwholesome ingredients and leave you less than satisfied, but Cali'flour's crusts are free of binders and unnatural substitute ingredients. They are low in carbs, high in protein, and contain only a few simple ingredients, with cauliflower always number one on the list.

Almost every day we hear from customers telling us how our pizza crusts have changed their lives. People like Jessee, who lost 165 pounds while eating Cali'flour crusts daily. Or three-year-old Eleanor, who has celiac disease and type 1 diabetes and is able to eat our crusts without a significant change in blood sugar. And touching stories like that of six-year-old Gavin, who has brain cancer and follows a ketogenic diet limited to 10 carbs daily. With our crusts,

Gavin gets to enjoy pizza just like any other kid. Our crusts allow people to claim a small part of their life back and experience happiness in the midst of hardship.

Our customers want to know how we do it. They've been begging for our top-secret, coveted crust recipe. We've listened, and in this book, we will be revealing our recipes for the first time ever! We've even included a bonus recipe for our Paleo Cali'flour Crust, not yet available commercially as of this writing. I'll take you step by step through our basic, Paleo, and Plant-Based DIY crust recipes. After you make them once, you'll marvel at how simple it is! A whole chapter on **Sauces, Spreads, and Cheeses** is the first step to putting together your pizzas and other Cali'flour creations. But the book goes way beyond pizza.

To start, the **Breakfast and Brunch** chapter includes all our favorites, from bagels to pancakes and porridge. One of the most popular ways of repurposing our crusts is to make them into sandwiches: The **Sandwiches and Toasts** chapter shows you how to slice and top your crusts with cashew cheese, as well as how to convert them into BLTs, avocado toast, crostini, and more. **Soups and Salads** features cauliflower as a creamy soup base and refreshing salad, like our take on the Italian bread salad known as panzanella. The **Cauliflower Rice** chapter swaps out grains so that comfort foods such as grits, burrito bowls, and mash are in reach for many of us again. One of the most clever repurposings of our crusts is as lasagna, which is part of the **Skillets, Casseroles, and Sheet Pans** chapter along with quiche, shepherd's pie, enchilada casserole, and cauliflower steaks. Cauliflower delights in the **Small Bites and Party Food** chapter, where you'll sneak cauliflower into hummus, lick your fingers with Buffalo cauliflower, and munch on cauliflower popcorn. Chapters dedicated to **Veggie Pizzas**, **Meaty Pizzas**, and **Seafood Pizzas** complete cauliflower's savory journey. We'll finish up with **Sweet Treats**, including a chile chocolate pie, my Nana's chocolate chip cookies, and coconut macaroons.

Our crusts are endlessly adaptable and welcome your imagination to turn our blank canvas into pizzas, sandwiches, salads, and more of your own creation! All of the recipes are gluten-free, grain-free, soy-free, and refined sugar–free. We've included dietary categories—gluten-free, grain-free, paleo, keto, keto friendly, vegan, vegetarian, dairy-free—for each recipe, with swaps that broaden the reach of the recipes so there's truly something for everyone. See page 230 to learn more about these diets.

Welcome to the wonderful world of cauliflower, and meet your new food soulmate! Get ready to indulge, because every recipe in this book is a trimmed-down, lower-carb version of the original food without a single gram of guilt! Every minute, twenty-one thousand slices of pizza are eaten in this country. That's more than a million per hour! What will your slice be?

Share your love story with us at www.califlourfoods.com, or tag us @califlourfoods on Facebook, Twitter, and Instagram. Happy cooking and eating!

Why Cauliflower?

Cauliflower is a rising superstar crucifer, and it's here to stay. It started with cauliflower steak and has continued with everything from bagels to cookies, popcorn, and rice. Pizza is cauliflower's greatest magic trick ever, as it loads up this crave-worthy comfort food with veggie love without leaving a clue that it's there. Because it's packed with nutrients, a cauliflower base for pizza isn't like the typical gluten-free replacement food containing additives, fillers, and tons of starch. Instead it's a nourishing companion to a low-carb diet. At Cali'flour Foods, we like to call it the new white flour! The benefits of a low-carb diet include lasting weight and fat loss, clearer thinking, fewer cravings, decreased inflammation, and lower risk for type 2 diabetes and heart disease. All that, and you get to eat pizza! People following just about every way of eating, including vegetarian, vegan, gluten-free, grain-free, paleo, and keto diets, as well as those of us who eat everything, can enjoy cauliflower pizza.

Is cauliflower the new kale? While kale is tasty tossed with Caesar dressing as a pizza topping or crunched as a chip, cauliflower's mild flavor and ability to act like flour offer endless opportunities that we've only begun to uncover. Imagine blending kale (or turnips, Brussels sprouts, or most any other vegetable) into a pizza crust and you get the picture. Cauliflower is a chameleon in the vegetable world, as it takes on the taste of anything it's cooked with.

Not only is cauliflower a culinary champion; it is one of the healthiest foods you can eat. Cauliflower is part of the crucifer family that includes arugula, broccoli, bok choy, Brussels sprouts, cabbage, collard greens, kale, Swiss chard, and turnips. All crucifers have powerful antioxidant and anticancer properties.

One cup of raw cauliflower is low in calories but contains significant amounts of vitamin C, vitamin K, vitamin B_6, thiamin, riboflavin, niacin, folate, pantothenic acid, potassium, manganese, magnesium, and phosphorus. Cauliflower leaves are particularly high in iron and calcium.

Inflammation is at the core of most chronic disease, and cauliflower's anti-inflammatory compounds are at the heart of its nutritional profile. Cauliflower is high in a host of antioxidants including beta-carotene, quercetin, rutin, and caffeic acid. It contains 77 percent of the recommended daily value of vitamin C to help fight everything from the common cold to cancer. Cauliflower contains sulforaphane, an antioxidant that has also been shown to kill cancer stem cells as well as protect against heart disease and diabetes. Cauliflower's carotenoid and flavonoid antioxidants have shown promise in their cancer-fighting abilities as well. Cauliflower can help us detox, thanks to its sulfur-containing glucosinolates, which support the removal of toxins from our body, keep out bad bacteria, and encourage good bacteria in our digestive systems.

Cauliflower florets kind of resemble the brain, so perhaps it's not a coincidence that cauliflower is brain food. It is one of the best plant-based sources of choline, an essential nutrient responsible for brain development that many people are deficient in. It's crucial during pregnancy, and a deficiency of choline may put us at higher risk for dementia and Alzheimer's disease later in life. The vitamin K it contains also can help keep your mind sharp as you age.

That 1 cup (110 g) of cauliflower contains a significant amount of fiber, which is 10 percent of our daily needs. The fiber protects us from conditions ranging from constipation to cancer, and it helps you feel full for longer. Cauliflower's slim calorie count makes it a friend to weight loss, and you get to eat more food without breaking the calorie bank!

Cauliflower is a blank slate to have fun in the kitchen with, and creative cooks can make use of every part of the vegetable, from the florets to the leaves. Cauliflower comes in white, yellow, green, and purple for visual diversity. Cauliflower has changed my life in so many ways, from bringing pizza night back to my house to creating a multi-million-dollar new food product category. If cauliflower can become a pizza, you, my friend, can become anything!

Setting Up Your Cali'flour Kitchen

Making Cali'flour Crusts at home is an easy DIY project that anyone can accomplish without special cooking skills. The crusts are so easy to shape that your kids can join in, and they'll feel a sense of accomplishment that they had a hand in making their meal. Few tools are required, and it's likely that you already have many of them in your kitchen.

Equipment

BAKING SHEETS You might want two to make multiple pizzas. You'll also need them for making cookies and other sweets (pages 224–229).

BLENDER For blending sauces, salsa, and spreads. A high-speed blender will give creamy sauces like White Sauce (page 44) the silkiest results.

BOWLS Of various sizes, for mixing your dough and everything else.

CAKE PAN (9-INCH/23-CM ROUND) For making lasagna (pages 136 and 138) and enchilada casserole (page 144).

CHEESECLOTH, NUT MILK BAG, OR THIN TEA TOWEL For squeezing out Cauliflower Meal (page 20). *Busy mom tip: I've also used a clean swaddling blanket!*

CHEESE GRATER For getting the cheese ready for crusts and for topping pizzas. You can also use the grater attachment of your food processor.

FOOD PROCESSOR For turning cauliflower into Cauliflower Rice (page 36) and Cauliflower Meal (page 20), pesto (pages 48–50), and a number of other recipes.

FREEZER BAGS For storing extra pizza crusts to enjoy later.

KNIVES AND CUTTING BOARDS The workhorses of the kitchen.

LOAF PAN (8 BY 4-INCH/20 BY 10-CM) For making the New White Bread (page 30).

MEASURING CUPS AND SPOONS Both dry and liquid measuring cups. An extra set of measuring spoons can come in handy.

MINI SPRAY BOTTLE OR ATOMIZER For citrus juice or vinegar. Optional, but they provide a fine, even misting to finish your pizzas.

PARCHMENT PAPER To place under your crusts. Do not use waxed paper, as it will stick to the crust.

PIE PAN (10-INCH/25-CM) For making quiche (page 140).

PIZZA PANS Circular mesh pizza pans for finishing your pizzas after adding toppings. You can find these in kitchen stores or online. If you don't have one, you can repurpose your baking pan.

VARIOUS TOOLS A pizza wheel, tongs, wooden spoons, peeler, rubber or silicone spatula, wide metal spatula, and 2½- to 3-inch (6- to 7.5-cm) cookie cutter for cutting out crostini.

Ingredients

You can find most ingredients in the supermarket or natural-foods store. If you don't, a quick online search will make every ingredient in the book available to you.

For making Cali'flour pizza crusts

BASIC CRUSTS call for three simple ingredients: cauliflower, eggs, and mozzarella cheese, all of which you'll find at any supermarket.

PLANT-BASED CRUSTS contain **nutritional yeast**, which you will find at natural-foods stores and some supermarkets. **Psyllium husk powder** can be found in the supplement section (if you can only find whole psyllium husks, grind them a bit finer before using). If you can't find **sesame seed flour** and **sunflower seed flour** in the store, look for them online, or grind small amounts of the seeds in a spice grinder or larger amounts in a food processor.

PALEO CRUSTS call for **almond flour, coconut flour,** and **ground chia seed**; these are all available at natural-foods stores and some supermarkets.

For the recipes

Note that all of the recipes in the book are gluten-free, grain-free, soy-free, bean-free, refined sugar–free, and unprocessed. To make sure your ingredients don't stray, read labels closely. Here are some things to look for:

ALMOND BUTTER Choose a no-sugar-added brand.

AVOCADO OIL Look for the word *unrefined* on the label, as otherwise it may be a processed oil.

BACON Look for nitrate- and nitrite-free and sugar-free bacon; brands labeled *paleo* should fit the bill.

CHOCOLATE Look for brands without refined sugar, or a stevia-sweetened chocolate such as Lily's.

COCONUT AMINOS A gluten- and soy-free substitute for soy sauce made from coconut sap.

COCONUT (DRIED) Choose a no-sugar-added brand.

COCONUT MILK My recipes call for full-fat unsweetened coconut milk from the can.

DAIRY Favor rBGH-free dairy without hormones; my recipes use full-fat dairy.

GRAIN-FREE NOODLES For people following a grain-free diet, pay particular attention to labels, as some bean-based noodles also contain a grain.

MAYONNAISE Look for 100 percent extra-virgin olive oil mayonnaise or unrefined avocado oil mayonnaise without added sugar or additives; brands labeled *paleo* should fit the bill.

PROBIOTIC POWDER Used to ferment the nut cheeses; look for dairy-free probiotics to keep your cheeses dairy-free.

SAUSAGE Look for nitrate- and nitrite-free, gluten-free, and sugar-free brands; sausage labeled *paleo* should fit the bill.

STEVIA Use unflavored stevia from a dropper bottle (powdered stevia often contains powdered whey and additives, and liquid is easier to measure in tiny amounts).

TAPIOCA FLOUR A grain-free starch used in several of the recipes.

TOMATO PRODUCTS Look for tomato paste, sauce, and other tomato products with no added sugar, high-fructose corn syrup, or additives.

VANILLA EXTRACT Look for purc vanilla extract, as otherwise it may be a petroleum-based product.

WORCESTERSHIRE SAUCE Look for *gluten-free* on the label, as many brands contain wheat.

If you decide to buy our crusts rather than go DIY, go to www.califlourfoods.com to stock up. All the crusts in the book can be ordered online and can be stored for up to nine months in your freezer for a quick and easy base for your creations. Remember, it may be our canvas, but it is your masterpiece!

PLEASE VISIT CALIFLOURFOODS.COM FOR A NUTRITIONAL PROFILE ON EACH RECIPE.

basics

Ever since the first Cali'flour pizza crusts hit the market, people have been asking me for my recipes on a daily basis. Until now they have been a closely guarded secret, so sharing them here is a big moment for me! And to sweeten the deal, I'm including our Paleo crust recipe as well, which as of this writing is not yet available in stores. All of the crusts have Italian Seasoning and Spicy Jalapeño versions just like our product. With every crust my intention has been to accommodate as many different ways of eating healthier as possible. This way there is a better chance that there is something here for everyone. The chapter also contains your new go-to white bread, cauliflower rice, chips, crackers, and breadcrumbs to complete your Cali'flour kitchen!

cali'flour meal

MAKES ABOUT 10 OUNCES (280 G/2 CUPS LOOSELY CRUMBLED) CAULIFLOWER MEAL (ENOUGH FOR 2 CRUSTS)

GLUTEN-FREE
GRAIN-FREE
PALEO
KETO FRIENDLY
VEGAN
VEGETARIAN
DAIRY-FREE

This is where cauliflower's magical transformation from whole head to pizza, quesadillas, lasagna, crackers, chips, breadcrumbs, and more begins. First we remove the core and leaves (don't toss them!), then we blend the florets to a smooth mashed potato consistency, bake the mash to release excess moisture, then squeeze the heck out of it to turn it into cauliflower meal, the base for our Cali'flour pizza crusts.

The recipe effortlessly scales up to get you ready for pizza night or to make multiple crusts to freeze and use later. I call for a 3-pound (1.4-kg) cauliflower, because it makes enough meal for two crusts, but of course you could use any size cauliflower and portion 5 ounces (140 g) of the meal for each crust. Note: Weighing is the most accurate way to measure your meal. If you do measure the meal by volume, loosely crumble it into the measuring cup (do not pack it in). Each head of cauliflower is unique, and two heads of the same weight can yield a slightly different amount of meal. If you have a small amount of meal left over, consider using it to make the New White Bread (page 30) or Coconut Macaroons (page 228).

Using a food processor will give you the most reliable results, but you could also use a high-speed blender. If you're using a Vitamix, continuously push down on the florets with the tamper to reach the desired consistency—this will take a bit of muscle and you may be left with some small pieces the size of rice or a little larger remaining; they will give your crusts rustic-looking texture!

1 (3-pound/1.4-kg) head cauliflower

Preheat the oven to 350°F (175°C) and line a baking sheet with parchment paper.

Cut the cauliflower (page 22, figure 1) into quarters through the core (figure 2), then cut out the core and leaves from each quarter in one cut (figure 3). Trim any remaining core and leaves (it's OK to leave a little of the stems from the cauliflower attached to the florets) (figure 4).

Break the cauliflower into approximately 2-inch (5-cm) florets (figure 5). It's OK if they are a little bigger or smaller—it's more important that they be more or less equal in size. Put half of the cauliflower in a food processor (figure 6) and process, stopping to scrape the sides of the bowl with a spatula a few times, until the cauliflower is uniformly broken down to the texture

1

2

3

4

5

6
ON
OFF-PULSE

7
ON
OFF-PULSE

8
ON
OFF-PULSE

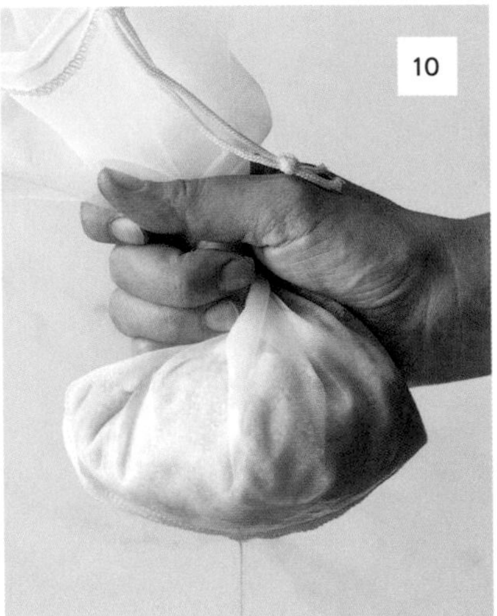

of wet sand (figure 7). You might be tempted to stop here, but keep on going. Continue to process, stopping to scrape the sides of the bowl with a spatula a few times, until the blade easily moves the mixture around to create a wet, smooth, creamy mashed potato texture with little flecks (figure 8). If any chunks larger than a green pea remain from the first batch (check by spreading the first batch over the baking sheet and running your fingers through it), add them to the second batch. Repeat with the remaining cauliflower.

Spread the cauliflower on the prepared baking sheet in an even layer (figure 9) and bake for 15 minutes. The object of baking is to release moisture from the cauliflower without browning it. There won't be much of a visual change—if it starts to brown, remove it from the oven immediately. Cool the cauliflower on the sheet completely.

Put about one quarter of the cauliflower meal in a nut milk bag or wrap it in four layers of cheesecloth (figure 10). Twist, then wring the liquid out over a bowl or the sink. Break the soon-to-be meal apart, then twist again until it is as dry as you can get it. Repeat this four or five times, until you can't squeeze out any more liquid. If your wrist starts to get tired, that's a good sign. Think of it as a mini arm workout! Expect to drain up to 2 cups (480 ml) liquid (the amount will vary for each batch). You should be able to form the final product into a smooth round that can crumble somewhat easily but still hold its form fairly well, like soft clay (figure 11). Use as directed in your recipe, or cover and refrigerate immediately (cauliflower meal starts to turn very quickly when left out). It will keep in the refrigerator for up to 3 days. Do not freeze.

Don't leave out the cauliflower leaves and stems

Did you know that 20 percent of the food we buy never gets eaten? Close to 100 percent of cauliflower leaves and stems suffer a similar fate because we are uninformed about how tasty, versatile, and nutritious these kitchen "scraps" are. Follow my lead and make creative use of the leaves by adding them to stir-fries, soups, and salads. You'll also find them in my Cauliflower Leaf Pesto (page 48), Shrimp and Cauliflower Leaf Grits (page 124), and Cauliflower Steak with Cauliflower Leaves (page 146). The leaves and stems have their own unique flavor, bright with fairly strong vegetal notes, so you only need a small amount to make their presence known. They are a great source of calcium, and their overall nutritional profile rivals that of the rest of the head (see page 14).

diy cali'flour pizza crusts

Once your cauliflower meal is made, forming and cooking cauliflower crusts is a cinch to accomplish. I recommend making multiple crusts at a time and freezing them to always have one on hand. They keep frozen for up to nine months.

For reliably consistent results, weigh your cauliflower meal using a digital scale rather than measuring it by volume. Feel free to make crusts of any size or shape: square crusts for sandwiches, small circles for crostini, tartlets, or mini pizzas. Have fun with it! If your pizza recipe doesn't require reheating (as with a salad pizza, for example), bake it a few minutes longer than indicated in the recipe.

TIP

Trace the bottom of a 9-inch (23-cm) round baking pan onto a sheet of parchment paper. Flip the parchment and use the circle as a guide for forming your crusts.

cali'flour pizza crust

MAKES 1 (9-INCH/23-CM) CRUST

GLUTEN FREE | GRAIN-FREE | KETO | VEGETARIAN

Three simple ingredients go into the recipe that launched the Cali'flour Crust and the cauliflower crust pizza movement in 2015. Many hours and changes along the way have made this award-winning crust what it is today.

- 5 ounces (140 g/1 cup loosely crumbled) Cauliflower Meal (page 20)
- ½ cup (55 g) shredded low-moisture whole milk mozzarella cheese (not fresh)
- 1 large egg

Preheat the oven to 350°F (175°C) and line a baking sheet with parchment paper.

In a medium bowl, combine all the ingredients and mix with a rubber spatula to incorporate (figures 1 and 2, opposite). Form the dough into a disc shape, then using your hands, press the dough out onto the prepared baking sheet to form an even 9-inch (23-cm) circle (figure 3). Place in the oven and bake for about 30 minutes, until firm and lightly browned (figure 4). Remove from the oven and use a metal spatula to slide the crust onto a wire rack to cool before adding your toppings. If you're not using the crust right away, store in a zip-top freezer bag in the freezer for up to 9 months. Do not refrigerate.

VARIATIONS

Italian Seasoning: *Add 1 teaspoon dried basil and 1 teaspoon garlic powder to the dough.*

Spicy Jalapeño: *Add 1 to 2 tablespoons minced jalapeño chile, 1¼ teaspoons red pepper flakes, and ¼ teaspoon garlic powder to the dough.*

1

2

3

4

plant-based cali'flour pizza crust

MAKES 1 (9-INCH/23-CM) CRUST

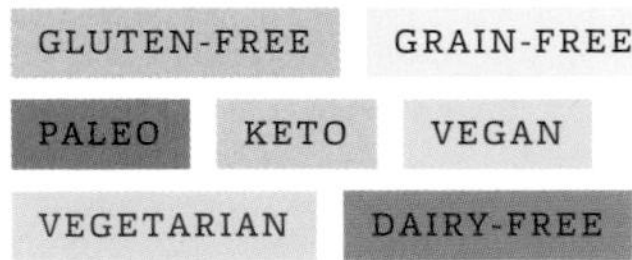

I attend food shows regularly, and one of the biggest trends I've seen is in plant-based foods. Another trend is high-protein, and both are here to stay. New products are coming out daily and paving a new way of eating clean. I created this pizza crust for our customers who asked for a dairy-free and egg-free pizza option. The first version of the recipe contained almond flour and flax, but recently we went back to the test kitchen and tweaked it to swap the nuts for seeds so folks with nut allergies can enjoy our pizza, too.

As it's not only gluten-free but grain-free, dairy-free, and full of protein, it is truly unlike any other cauliflower pizza crust on the market! In fact, it has won two Clean Eating awards nationwide.

If you'd like to make your own sesame seed flour and sunflower seed flour, grind small amounts in a spice grinder or larger amounts in a food processor.

TIP

Make sure not to overgrind your seeds, or you will end up with nut butter (which, of course, you can spread over a crust and call it a sandwich).

¼ cup (25 g) sesame seed flour

¼ cup (25 g) sunflower seed flour

2 teaspoons nutritional yeast

1½ teaspoons psyllium husk powder

¼ teaspoon sea salt

5 ounces (140 g/1 cup loosely crumbled) Cauliflower Meal (page 20)

1 tablespoon extra-virgin olive oil

Preheat the oven to 350°F (175°C) and line a baking sheet with parchment paper.

In a medium bowl, whisk together the sesame seed flour, sunflower seed flour, nutritional yeast, psyllium powder, and salt. Crumble in the cauliflower meal, add the oil, and mix with a rubber spatula to incorporate. Switch to your hands and knead for about 30 seconds, until well combined and a homogenous dough is formed. Form the dough into a disc shape, then using your hands, press the dough out onto the prepared baking sheet to form an even 9-inch (23-cm) circle. Place in the oven and bake for about 30 minutes, until firm and lightly browned. Remove from the oven and use a metal spatula to slide the crust onto a wire rack to cool before adding your toppings. If you're not using the crust right away, store in a zip-top freezer bag in the freezer for up to 9 months. Do not refrigerate.

VARIATIONS

Italian Seasoning: *Add 1 teaspoon dried basil and ½ teaspoon garlic powder to the dough.*

Spicy Jalapeño: *Reduce the salt to ⅛ teaspoon and add 1 to 2 tablespoons minced jalapeño chile, 1¼ teaspoons red pepper flakes, and ¼ teaspoon garlic powder to the dough.*

paleo cali'flour pizza crust

MAKES 1 (9-INCH/23-CM) CRUST

GLUTEN-FREE GRAIN-FREE

PALEO KETO-FRIENDLY

VEGETARIAN DAIRY-FREE

The elusive and formerly daunting Paleo pizza crust is no longer just a concept but a reality and just as easy to put together as the basic and Plant-Based crusts. While many paleo baked goods add tapioca starch into the mix, I wanted to nix the extra carbs with this one. So not only does it meet the paleo standard, but it's keto as well!

2 tablespoons almond flour

2 tablespoons coconut flour

1 tablespoon ground chia seed (see Note)

½ teaspoon sea salt

2 large eggs

5 ounces (140 g/1 cup loosely crumbled) Cauliflower Meal (page 20)

Preheat the oven to 350°F (175°C) and line a baking sheet with parchment paper.

In a medium bowl, whisk together the almond flour, coconut flour, chia flour, and salt. Whisk in the eggs, then crumble in the cauliflower meal and mix with a rubber spatula to incorporate. Switch to your hands and knead for about 30 seconds, until well combined and a homogenous dough is formed. Form the dough into a disc shape, then using your hands, press the dough out onto the prepared baking sheet to form an even 9-inch (23-cm) circle. Place in the oven and bake for about 30 minutes, until firm and lightly browned. Remove from the oven and use a metal spatula to slide the crust onto a wire rack to cool before adding your toppings. If you're not using the crust right away, store in a zip-top freezer bag in the freezer for up to 9 months. Do not refrigerate.

NOTE: For most reliable results, use Spectrum ground chia seed.

VARIATIONS

Italian Seasoning: *Add 1 teaspoon dried basil and 1 teaspoon garlic powder to the dough.*

Spicy Jalapeño: *Add 1 to 2 tablespoons minced jalapeño chile, 1¼ teaspoons red pepper flakes, and ¼ teaspoon garlic powder to the dough.*

the new white bread

MAKES 1 (8-INCH/20-CM) LOAF (16 SLICES)

GLUTEN-FREE

GRAIN-FREE

PALEO

KETO

VEGETARIAN

This recipe comes to us from Doug Smith, of our research and development team, master of making keto-friendly foods taste as great as their non-keto counterparts! I grew up on white bread, but it was the kind we'd spread with butter and sugar, cut the crusts off, and roll into a ball before eating as an after-school snack (no wonder I became so inflamed!).

Because of the large amount of egg whites it contains, this bread holds together perfectly and is never dry or crumbly, as some gluten-free breads can be. It's perfect for French Toast (page 76), Croutons (page 33), and garlic toast (see variation, opposite), and to fill the breadbasket. Toast it before serving, as toasted is when it is at its very best.

- 6 large eggs, separated
- ¼ teaspoon cream of tartar
- 1¼ cups (140 g) almond flour
- 4 ounces (115 g/¾ cup loosely crumbled) Cauliflower Meal (page 20)
- ¼ cup (55 g) ghee or unsalted butter, melted and cooled
- 1 tablespoon baking powder
- 5 drops unflavored liquid stevia
- ⅛ teaspoon sea salt

Preheat the oven to 375°F (190°C) and line an 8 by 4-inch (20 by 10-cm) loaf pan with parchment paper.

Put the egg whites in a large bowl, add the cream of tartar, and beat with an electric hand mixer until firm peaks form.

In a food processor, combine the almond flour, cauliflower meal, egg yolks, ghee, baking powder, stevia, and salt and process to combine. Add about one-third of the beaten egg whites and pulse until smooth; do not overprocess. Transfer to a large bowl and gently fold in the remaining beaten egg whites one-third at a time, then pour into the prepared pan. Bake for 30 minutes, or until very lightly browned on top. Turn off the oven and crack the oven door open. Leave in the oven for 20 minutes, then remove from the oven, place on a wire rack, and cool completely in the pan. Remove the bread from the pan, slice, and serve. The bread will keep, wrapped in plastic wrap, for up to 5 days in the refrigerator and up to 1 month in the freezer.

SWAP

To make this bread dairy-free: Omit the ghee.

VARIATION

Garlic Toast: *Slice the bread and toast it. In a small skillet, melt 6 tablespoons (85 g) salted butter with 3 cloves garlic, pressed through a garlic press. Let sit for a few minutes, then brush over the bread. Or spread Roasted Garlic Cream (page 51) over the toast.*

1 TABLESPOON

croutons

MAKES ABOUT 1 CUP (30 G)

The best part of the salad now *is* salad. These croutons, made by toasting cubes of New White Bread on the stovetop, are Caesar-worthy (page 110) and a great topper to any soup or salad. They are best used right after you make them, but you can re-crisp them in a toaster oven if you have any left over.

1 tablespoon ghee or unsalted butter

¾ teaspoon minced fresh herbs such as thyme, oregano, or parsley, or a mixture

3 (½-inch/12-mm) slices New White Bread (page 30), cut into ½-inch (12-mm) cubes

⅛ teaspoon sea salt

Pinch of freshly ground black pepper

Melt the ghee in a medium skillet over medium heat. Add the herbs and cook, stirring constantly, for 15 seconds. Add the bread cubes and cook, stirring frequently, until well browned all over, 5 to 7 minutes. Add the salt and pepper and toss to coat. Let cool, then use in your recipe.

GLUTEN-FREE

GRAIN-FREE

PALEO*

KETO

VEGETARIAN

* If using ghee

cali'flour chips or crackers

SERVES 4

This recipe came from my right-hand woman at Cali'flour Foods, COO Jimi Sturgeon-Smith. Jimi is a dipping kind of girl. Make sure you take her to a restaurant that has mayo and ranch dressing, because the girl just loves a creamy sauce to dip into. She cuts up our crusts to turn them into chips just for that reason! Look for our sister product on the market, the low-carb cauliflower cracker, courtesy of Jimi.

If you're working from a frozen crust, cut it while still partially frozen for the neatest results. These are best used the day they are made, but if you have any left over, store them in a plastic bag or airtight container in the refrigerator and re-crisp in a toaster oven before serving.

2 Cali'flour pizza crusts, any type (pages 26–29)

Preheat the oven to 350°F (175°C) and line a baking sheet with parchment paper.

Cut the crusts into chip or cracker shapes, any size you like. Place on the prepared baking sheet and bake, turning once, until they are crispy and well browned, 12 to 15 minutes. Check frequently, as some pieces may cook faster than others and may need to be removed earlier. Remove from the oven, cool completely, and serve.

cali'flour breadcrumbs

MAKES ABOUT 1 CUP (100 G)

Many of my family's recipes, from chicken Parmesan to okra, revolved around breading and frying. I no longer like to fry anything, but I still like the comfort of breadcrumbs sprinkled over soups, salads, and dips or coating a piece of fish or chicken. A Cali'flour pizza crust baked, broken up, and whirled in the food processor is my solution. You can also make extra breadcrumbs with odd-shaped pieces of crust left over from stamping out circles for crostini (page 96).

1 Cali'flour pizza crust, any type (pages 26–29)

Preheat the oven to 375°F (190°C) and line a baking sheet with parchment paper.

Place the crust on the prepared baking sheet and bake, turning once, until crispy and well browned, about 12 minutes. Remove from the oven and cool completely, then break into chunks and pulse in a food processor to fine crumbs. Store in a covered container in the refrigerator for up to 5 days. Reheat in a hot pan or in the toaster oven for a couple of minutes to re-crisp them.

cauliflower rice

MAKES ABOUT 8 CUPS (2¼ POUNDS/1 KG)

GLUTEN-FREE
GRAIN-FREE
PALEO
KETO FRIENDLY
VEGAN
VEGETARIAN
DAIRY-FREE

Rice was a huge part of my life when I was growing up. It was also for my mom and her mom too, a reflection of our family's food reality in the tight times of the Depression. I have such fond memories of eating white rice with milk, cinnamon, and sugar at my grandma Netta's. While the memories will always be there, now when I eat regular rice, it triggers inflammation, so making the switch to cauliflower rice means I can once again eat not only porridge (page 68) but pancakes (page 64) and many other everyday dishes. And I can even enjoy rice bowls (pages 122, 126, and 130). Note that many cauliflower pizza recipes are based on cauliflower rice, but we use cauliflower meal (page 20) for ours.

1 (3-pound/1.4-kg) head cauliflower

Cut the cauliflower into quarters through the core, then cut out the core and leaves from each quarter in one cut. Trim any remaining core and leaves (it's OK to leave a little of the stems from the cauliflower attached to the florets).

Break the cauliflower into approximately 2-inch (5-cm) florets. It's OK if they are a little bigger or smaller—it's more important that they be more or less equal in size. Put half of the cauliflower in a food processor and pulse the florets 15 to 20 times, until the pieces are the size of grains of rice, scraping the sides of the machine once or twice and keeping in mind that it doesn't have to be perfect and likely will not be! If any large chunks remain, reserve them and pulse them in the second batch. Use as directed in your recipe, or immediately cover and refrigerate (cauliflower rice starts to turn very quickly when left out) for up to 3 days. Do not freeze.

Cuisinart
DLC-7
METAL BLADE
ON
OFF-PULSE

sauces, spreads, and cheeses

I'm a huge sauce person. I love dipping, spreading, and putting a little something on just about everything. When I lived in Louisiana, I learned the word *lagniappe*, which means something extra special, like a bonus or gift. That's what sauces are to me, and Louisiana is where my palate for fine dining and sauces in particular came from. And, of course, you can't have pizza without sauce. So I've shared some of my favorites, from standard marinara and Bolognese to cauliflower white sauce, salsa, cauliflower leaf pesto, and three plant-based cheeses to go with. I've got your pizzas and everything else covered!

marinara sauce

MAKES ABOUT 3 CUPS (720 ML)

GLUTEN-FREE
GRAIN-FREE
PALEO
KETO FRIENDLY
VEGAN
VEGETARIAN
DAIRY-FREE

You can't make a Margherita Pizza (page 162) without it, and it is a good friend to the Hawaiian Pizza (page 190), Stir-Fry-Style Pizza (page 182), and, of course, the classic Pepperoni Pizza (page 186). Consider freezing it in ¼-cup (60-ml) portions for convenience. Crushed tomatoes make a smooth marinara that spreads evenly over the crusts.

2 tablespoons extra-virgin olive oil

1 yellow onion, minced

2 cloves garlic, minced

¼ teaspoon dried oregano

¼ teaspoon red pepper flakes

1 (28-ounce/794-g) can crushed tomatoes

¾ teaspoon sea salt, or to taste

½ teaspoon freshly ground black pepper

1 tablespoon chopped fresh basil

Heat the oil in a medium saucepan over medium heat. Add the onion and cook until softened and starting to brown, about 5 minutes. Add the garlic and cook until fragrant, about 1 minute. Add the oregano and red pepper flakes and cook for 30 seconds. Add the tomatoes, salt, and pepper and bring to a simmer. Reduce the heat and cook uncovered until slightly thickened, about 30 minutes. Add the basil and remove from the heat. Use as directed in your recipe, or cool and store in a covered container in the refrigerator for up to 5 days or in the freezer for up to 2 months.

quick bolognese sauce

MAKES ABOUT 5 CUPS (1.2 L)

GLUTEN-FREE

GRAIN-FREE

PALEO*

KETO FRIENDLY

DAIRY-FREE

* If using beef stock

When I was growing up, my mom would make a big batch of Bolognese sauce, and I remember loving the leftovers for days after. It was something nourishing we could enjoy with pasta while keeping to our food budget. I also grew up listening to the music of Alan Jackson. I never would have imagined that one day I'd have Alan Jackson's daughter, Mattie Jackson, of Salt & Vine in Nashville, serving our crusts with her Bolognese sauce. This recipe is inspired by Mattie's creative use of our crusts. You can also make this sauce with veal, pork, lamb, turkey, or a combination. You might consider making extra and freezing it in ½-cup (120-ml) pizza-topping portions.

1 tablespoon extra-virgin olive oil

1 large onion, chopped

1 large rib celery, minced

1 large carrot, minced

3 cloves garlic, minced

1 pound (455 g) ground beef

1 teaspoon dried oregano

1 teaspoon dried basil

1 bay leaf

3 tablespoons tomato paste

½ cup (120 ml) dry red wine, white wine, or beef stock

1 (28-ounce/794-g) can whole tomatoes with juices

½ teaspoon sea salt, or to taste

½ teaspoon freshly ground black pepper, or to taste

Heat the oil in a large saucepan over medium heat. Add the onion, celery, and carrot and cook until softened but not browned, about 5 minutes. Add the garlic and cook for 1 minute, or until aromatic. Add the beef and cook, stirring and breaking up large pieces as you go, for about 15 minutes, until it is no longer pink and well browned on the bottom of the pot. Stir in the oregano, basil, and bay leaf and cook for 1 minute. Add the tomato paste and cook, stirring, for 2 minutes. Stir in the wine, scraping the bottom of the pan, and cook until it is mostly evaporated, about 5 minutes. Add the whole tomatoes, crushing them with your hands directly into the pot, then add the tomato juices, salt, and pepper and bring to a simmer. Reduce the heat to low, cover, and cook for 45 minutes to 1 hour. Taste and add more salt and/or pepper if needed. Use as directed in your recipe, or cool and store in a covered container in the refrigerator for up to 5 days or in the freezer for up to 2 months.

quick bolognese sauce
white sauce

white sauce

MAKES ABOUT 1½ CUPS (360 ML)

GLUTEN-FREE

GRAIN-FREE

PALEO

KETO FRIENDLY

VEGAN

VEGETARIAN

DAIRY-FREE

One of my mom's regular dishes was tuna noodle casserole with white sauce. My mom was a hardworking woman, so tuna casserole was a delicious quick fix. But I have a version for you that can also be made in just a few minutes, and it's enriched with a mix of cauliflower, cashews, and coconut milk. It makes an oh-so-creamy dairy-free pizza topping (pages 213 and 214) and stars in a vegan take on alfredo sauce (pages 178 and 214).

- 2 cups chopped (1-inch/2.5-cm pieces) cauliflower florets and stems (about 8 ounces/225 g)
- ¼ cup (40 g) raw cashews
- 1 large clove garlic, peeled
- ¾ cup (180 ml) vegetable stock or water, plus more as needed
- ¼ cup (60 ml) canned unsweetened coconut milk
- ½ teaspoon sea salt
- 2 teaspoons nutritional yeast
- ½ teaspoon grated lemon zest
- 1½ teaspoons fresh lemon juice, or to taste
- ¼ teaspoon freshly ground white pepper
- 2 teaspoons chopped fresh herbs such as oregano and thyme

Combine the cauliflower, cashews, garlic, stock, coconut milk, and salt in a medium saucepan. Place over medium-high heat and bring to a simmer. Reduce the heat to medium-low, cover, and cook, stirring to keep the cauliflower and cashews coated in the liquid and mashing them slightly with the spoon, until the cauliflower and cashews are softened, about 10 minutes.

Transfer to a blender (preferably a high-speed blender) and let cool slightly. Add the nutritional yeast, lemon zest, lemon juice, and white pepper and blend until silky smooth. Add the herbs and pulse or stir them in. Taste and add more salt and/or lemon juice if needed and add more water or stock if it's too thick. Use immediately, or store in a covered container in the refrigerator for up to 3 days.

red salsa

MAKES ABOUT 1½ CUPS (360 ML)

Mexican food was a big part of growing up in California, and Mexican food brings back college memories. My roommates and I practically lived off it. So it comes as a natural that salsa, both red and green (page 46), have become partners to our crusts. And not only that but to nachos (page 156), burrito bowls (page 130), and more. Using canned tomatoes, which are picked at the peak of ripeness, enables you to make good salsa in any season. The tomatoes are roasted to concentrate their flavor and juices to make a salsa that's perfect for topping pizza crusts. For a juicier salsa, of the thickness for dipping chips into or topping a rice bowl, add some of the juices back from the can.

- 1 tablespoon extra-virgin olive oil
- 1 (28-ounce/794-g) can whole tomatoes, drained
- 2 cloves garlic, peeled
- ½ small white onion, chopped
- 1 large jalapeño chile, chopped
- 1 cup (40 g) chopped fresh cilantro
- 2 tablespoons fresh lime juice
- ⅛ teaspoon ground cumin
- ½ teaspoon sea salt

Preheat the oven to 450°F (230°C). Grease a medium ovenproof skillet or small baking sheet with the oil.

Pour the tomatoes and their juices through a mesh strainer set over a bowl. Break up the tomatoes with your hands to release more of their liquid; reserve the liquid. Place the tomatoes in the prepared skillet and roast, turning once or twice, until they are fairly dry, 10 to 15 minutes. Remove from the skillet and let cool.

In a food processor with the motor running, drop the garlic through the hole in the top to mince. Add the onion, chile, cilantro, lime juice, cumin, and salt and pulse until roughly chopped. Add the tomatoes and pulse until chopped. If the salsa looks too wet for spreading over a pizza, drain into a mesh strainer set over a bowl; if it looks too dry, add some of the reserved tomato juices. Transfer to a bowl and use in your recipe, or cover and refrigerate for up to 3 days.

GLUTEN-FREE
GRAIN-FREE
PALEO
KETO FRIENDLY
VEGAN
VEGETARIAN
DAIRY-FREE

green salsa

MAKES ABOUT 1½ CUPS (360 ML)

GLUTEN-FREE

GRAIN-FREE

PALEO

KETO FRIENDLY

VEGAN

VEGETARIAN

DAIRY-FREE

I love a good spicy green salsa! While Red Salsa (page 45) is deep and rich in flavor, green salsa offers a fresh, tart taste that lights up dishes from Avocado Toast (page 98) to Enchilada Casserole (page 144). Broiling the tomatillos gives the salsa deep smoky notes. If you can't decide which salsa to use, choose both, as I do for Huevos Divorciados (page 79). Tomatillos look like little green tomatoes that are wrapped in a papery husk. Peel off and discard the husk and rinse the tomatillos before making your salsa.

1 pound (455 g) tomatillos, husked and rinsed well

½ white onion, cut in half

1 large jalapeño chile, stemmed

2 cloves garlic, unpeeled

¾ teaspoon sea salt

½ cup (20 g) roughly chopped fresh cilantro leaves and stems

Preheat the broiler.

Place the tomatillos, onion, chile, and garlic on a baking sheet. Broil until the tomatillos, chile, and garlic are blackened in places and the tomatillos are softened and dulled in color, about 5 minutes. Remove the garlic if it is well browned at this point. Using tongs, turn everything over and broil for about 5 minutes on the other side, until the tomatillos collapse. Cool slightly, then peel the garlic. Transfer the roasted vegetables, including the juices from the tomatillos, to a blender or food processor. Add the salt and blend until it breaks down into a rough puree, adding a little water if it's too thick, then add the cilantro and pulse to combine. Transfer to a bowl and use in your recipe, or cover and refrigerate for up to 3 days.

VARIATION

Toasted Árbol Chile Green Salsa: *Remove the stems from 1 or 2 dried árbol chiles. Toast them in a skillet over medium-high heat for about 2 minutes on each side, until darkened in color. Cool completely, then crumble the toasted chiles into the blender with the salsa and blend to combine.*

green salsa
red salsa

cauliflower leaf pesto

MAKES ABOUT 1 CUP (240 ML)

GLUTEN-FREE

GRAIN-FREE

KETO

VEGETARIAN

Heroic hours of grinding, baking, and squeezing of cauliflower florets went into testing the recipes in this book. In order to make use of the mountains of leaves left behind, one of my testers, Katie Eyles, came up with this take on pesto. Cauliflower leaves add bright, slightly bitter vegetal notes, transforming pesto into a new classic companion to our crusts. Note that only a small amount of the leaves is needed for flavor, and you'll be using just the green parts of the leaves, not the white crispy parts. If you don't have cauliflower leaves handy, swap in more basil or another herb.

3 cloves garlic, peeled

¼ cup (35 g) pine nuts

¼ teaspoon sea salt, or to taste

¼ teaspoon freshly ground black pepper, or to taste

1 teaspoon grated lemon zest

1 tablespoon fresh lemon juice, or to taste

¼ cup (25 g) grated Parmesan cheese

½ cup (10 g) cauliflower leaves (just the green parts)

1½ cups (60 g) packed fresh basil leaves and tender stems

3 tablespoons chopped fresh parsley leaves and tender stems

6 to 8 tablespoons (90 to 120 ml) extra-virgin olive oil

In a food processor with the motor running, drop the garlic through the hole in the top to mince. Add the pine nuts, salt, and pepper and process until coarsely ground. Add the lemon zest, lemon juice, cheese, cauliflower leaves, basil, and parsley and process to mince the greens. With the motor still running, drizzle in the oil through the hole in the top to incorporate. If the mixture is too thick, add a little water. Transfer to a container, cover, and store in the refrigerator for up to 1 week or in the freezer for up to 3 months.

cauliflower leaf pesto
plant-based pesto

plant-based pesto

MAKES ABOUT 1 CUP (240 ML)

GLUTEN-FREE
GRAIN-FREE
PALEO
KETO
VEGAN
VEGETARIAN
DAIRY-FREE

Like our cheese-containing Cauliflower Leaf Pesto (page 48), the plant-based version is made with cauliflower leaves to add an unexpected crucifer component. Note that only a small amount is needed for their unique flavor, and you'll be using just the green parts of the leaves, not the white crispy parts. If you don't have cauliflower leaves, swap in more basil or another herb. And feel free to use other nuts or seeds, such as pine nuts, sunflower seeds, or macadamias.

3 cloves garlic, peeled

¼ cup (25 g) walnut halves

¼ cup (35 g) hulled pumpkin seeds

¾ teaspoon sea salt, or to taste

¼ teaspoon freshly ground black pepper, or to taste

1 teaspoon grated lemon zest

1 tablespoon fresh lemon juice, or to taste

½ cup (10 g) cauliflower leaves (just the green parts)

1½ cups (60 g) packed fresh basil leaves and tender stems

¼ cup (10 g) chopped fresh cilantro leaves and tender stems

6 to 8 tablespoons (90 to 120 ml) extra-virgin olive oil

In a food processor with the motor running, drop the garlic through the hole in the top to mince. Add the walnuts, pumpkin seeds, salt, and pepper and process until coarsely ground. Add the lemon zest, lemon juice, cauliflower leaves, basil, and cilantro and process to mince the greens. With the motor still running, drizzle in the oil through the hole in the top to incorporate. If the mixture is too thick, add a little water. Transfer to a container, cover, and store in the refrigerator for up to 1 week or in the freezer for up to 3 months.

roasted garlic cream

MAKES ABOUT ½ CUP (120 ML)

Garlic is a potent antioxidant: It reduces inflammation, strengthens immunity, and can even protect against cancer. Roasting it concentrates nutrition, with each tablespoon of garlic cream containing a whopping half a head of garlic. That's great news, because what isn't better with more garlic? Spread a little over a crust before adding sauce for an extra layer of flavor, use it to make the best keto-friendly garlic toast ever (page 31), or spread liberally on Detox Pizza (page 168) to cleanse while you enjoy your slice! Feel free to change up the herbs and double the recipe to freeze some for later.

4 heads garlic

5 teaspoons extra-virgin olive oil

½ teaspoon minced fresh rosemary

½ teaspoon minced fresh thyme

Large pinch of sea salt

Pinch of freshly ground black pepper

Preheat the oven to 375°F (190°C).

Remove the papery outer layers from the garlic bulbs and cut off ½ inch (12 mm) from the top, leaving the bulbs intact. Place the garlic cut-side up on a large piece of aluminum foil and drizzle the cut part of each bulb with 1 teaspoon of the oil. Tightly wrap the garlic in the foil and bake for about 45 minutes, until the garlic is completely softened and lightly colored. Cool to room temperature, then gently squeeze the root end of the bulbs to squeeze out the cloves. Any cloves that don't pop out can be squeezed out individually.

Put the garlic cloves in a medium bowl. Add the remaining 1 teaspoon oil, the rosemary, thyme, salt, and pepper and mash with the back of a fork to form a paste. The garlic cream will keep in the refrigerator for up to 1 week or in the freezer for up to 1 month.

GLUTEN-FREE

GRAIN-FREE

PALEO

KETO FRIENDLY

VEGAN

VEGETARIAN

DAIRY-FREE

creamy tahini sauce

MAKES ABOUT 1 CUP (240 ML)

GLUTEN-FREE
GRAIN-FREE
PALEO
KETO
VEGAN
VEGETARIAN
DAIRY-FREE

Tahini sauce, a Middle Eastern condiment based on sesame seeds, olive oil, garlic, and lemon, plays well not only with hummus but also Avocado Toast (page 98), turkey sandwiches (page 94), and, of course, pizza. If you're using the sauce for a salad, thin it out with a little water. This recipe is based on one my coauthor, Leda Scheintaub, and her husband, Nash Patel, use at their Brattleboro, Vermont, food truck, Dosa Kitchen. Dosas are light, crispy crepes, and I love them because they're not only delicious but, like our crusts, gluten-free. If you're ever in the area, be sure to order their falafel dosa with tahini sauce. You won't be disappointed!

- ⅔ cup (165 ml) tahini (sesame paste)
- ¼ cup (60 ml) extra-virgin olive oil
- 2 teaspoons grated lime zest
- ¼ cup fresh lime juice, or to taste
- 2 cloves garlic, halved
- ½ teaspoon sea salt, or to taste
- ¼ teaspoon freshly ground black pepper
- 2 tablespoons finely chopped fresh flat-leaf parsley

In a blender, combine 6 tablespoons (90 ml) water with all the ingredients except the parsley and blend until smooth. Add more water if needed to thin it. Add the parsley and pulse until just combined. Taste and add more lime juice and/or salt if needed. Store in a covered container in the refrigerator for up to 1 week.

roasted garlic cream
creamy tahini sauce
white bean spread

white bean spread

MAKES ABOUT 1½ CUPS (360 ML)

GLUTEN-FREE

GRAIN-FREE

KETO FRIENDLY

VEGAN

VEGETARIAN

DAIRY-FREE

You can make a decent bean spread by simply opening up a can of beans and blending them. But taking a few minutes to cook the beans with garlic, onion, and herbs rewards you with a full-flavored spread that adds a creamy element to pizza crusts and sandwiches. Or serve it solo with a drizzle of oil, a squeeze of lemon, salt, and pepper as a dip for Cali'flour Chips (page 34). Change up the herbs with whatever you have, from marjoram to oregano and parsley. The flavors will change as the dip sits, so take another taste just before serving.

- 4 tablespoons (60 ml) extra-virgin olive oil
- ½ small onion, finely chopped
- 2 cloves garlic, minced
- 2 teaspoons red wine vinegar, or to taste
- 1½ teaspoons minced fresh herbs such as thyme or rosemary
- 1 (15-ounce/430-g) can cannellini beans, drained and rinsed
- ½ teaspoon sea salt, or to taste
- ¼ teaspoon freshly ground black pepper, or to taste

In a medium saucepan, heat 1 tablespoon of the oil over medium heat. Add the onion and cook until softened, about 5 minutes. Add the garlic and cook until fragrant, about 1 minute. Add 1 teaspoon of the vinegar and stir for 10 seconds. Add the herbs, beans, and ½ cup (120 ml) water and cook for 5 minutes, or until the water is absorbed. Transfer to a blender or food processor, add the remaining 3 tablespoons oil, an additional 2 tablespoons water, the remaining 1 teaspoon vinegar, the salt, and pepper, and blend until smooth. Add more water if the mixture is too thick. Taste and add more salt, pepper, and/or vinegar if needed. Serve immediately, or cool, cover, and store in the refrigerator for up to 3 days.

VARIATION

Black Bean Spread: *Sub black beans for the white.*

plant-based parmesan cheese

MAKES ABOUT 1¼ CUPS (145 G)

Ounce for ounce, macadamia nuts have the highest amount of fat of any nut, making this cheese perfect for those following a keto diet and great for the rest of us who value quality plant-based fats in our diets. Wherever you fall on the plant-based spectrum, you're going to want to have this cheese in your fridge at all times! If there are any large pieces of nuts remaining after processing them, pick them out and enjoy them rather than risk overprocessing and turning your macadamia cheese into macadamia butter (but if you do, you certainly could make sandwiches with it!).

- 1 cup (135 g) raw macadamia nuts
- 2 tablespoons nutritional yeast
- ¾ teaspoon sea salt

In a small food processor, combine all the ingredients and pulse until the nuts are broken down into a crumbly grated-Parm texture. Cover and store in the refrigerator for up to 1 month.

GLUTEN-FREE

GRAIN-FREE

PALEO

KETO

VEGAN

VEGETARIAN

DAIRY-FREE

plant-based parmesan cheese
cashew cream cheese

ALMOND RICOTTA VARIATION

Herb Ricotta: *Add 2 tablespoons finely chopped herbs such as rosemary, thyme, oregano, marjoram, or a combination after the cheese is fermented.*

CASHEW CREAM CHEESE VARIATIONS

Herb Cashew Cream Cheese: *Add 2 teaspoons finely chopped herbs such as rosemary, thyme, oregano, marjoram, or a combination after the cheese is fermented.*

Cinnamon Cashew Cream Cheese: *Whisk in ½ teaspoon ground cinnamon after the cheese is fermented.*

almond ricotta

MAKES ABOUT 3 CUPS (720 ML)

GLUTEN-FREE
GRAIN-FREE
PALEO
KETO
VEGAN
VEGETARIAN
DAIRY-FREE

The plant-based people's dream cheese: It's so easy to make, and fermenting it infuses it with probiotics, which are friendly bacteria that promote good digestion and overall gut health. Probiotics help us to absorb nutrients and fight infections, and they can even help lift your mood and fight depression. Fermentation time varies widely depending on kitchen temperature and the air circulation in your kitchen, so taste after six hours and then taste periodically until it is tangy to your liking. Because the benefits of probiotics are destroyed from cooking, add ricotta just before serving your pizza or other dishes.

Purchase probiotic powder from the refrigerator case in the supplement section of your natural foods store; if unavailable, simply empty out probiotic capsules. Make sure the probiotics are dairy-free to keep the ricotta dairy-free.

2 cups (285 g) raw almonds
1 teaspoon probiotic powder
¼ teaspoon sea salt

Put the almonds in a medium bowl and add water to cover. Cover with a dish towel and soak for at least 6 hours or up to 12 hours. Drain.

Bring a medium pot of water to a boil. Add the almonds and leave for 10 seconds, then drain. Cool slightly, then pop the skins off the almonds by squeezing them between your thumb and pointer finger.

Put the almonds, 1 cup (240 ml) water, the probiotic powder, and salt in a blender (preferably a high-speed blender) and blend until mostly smooth with a little texture remaining but no large chunks of almonds.

Place a mesh strainer over a bowl and line with enough cheesecloth to cover the almond mixture (or use a nut milk bag). Gather the almond mixture in the cheesecloth, making sure it covers it completely, then cover with a small plate. Place a weight such as a can of beans or tomatoes on the plate and leave to drain for at least 6 hours or up to 24 hours depending on how warm your kitchen is and how tangy you like your ricotta. Remove the cheese from the cheesecloth, put it into a container, cover, and refrigerate for up to 2 weeks.

cashew cream cheese

MAKES ABOUT 1 CUP (225 G)

Like the Almond Ricotta (page 58), this plant-based cheese is fermented using probiotic powder to give it some serious zing! Taste after two days, and then taste periodically until it is tangy to your liking. Purchase probiotic powder from the refrigerator case of the supplement section of your natural foods store; if unavailable, empty out probiotic capsules. Make sure the probiotics are dairy-free to keep the cream cheese dairy-free.

1½ cups (195 g) raw cashews
1 teaspoon probiotic powder
½ teaspoon sea salt

Put the cashews in a medium bowl and add hot water to cover. Cover with a dish towel and soak for at least 2 hours or up to 12 hours. Drain.

In a small high-speed blender or food processor, combine the cashews, ¼ cup (60 ml) water, the probiotic powder, and salt and blend until very smooth, 3 to 5 minutes, stopping to scrape the sides of the machine a couple of times and adding a little more water if needed if it's too thick. Place in a jar or container, loosely cover, and leave out to ferment for 2 to 3 days, stirring once or twice a day to keep a skin from forming on top. The cream cheese will keep, covered, in the refrigerator for up to 2 weeks.

GLUTEN-FREE
GRAIN-FREE
PALEO
KETO
VEGAN*
VEGETARIAN
DAIRY-FREE

* If vegan probiotic powder is used

breakfast and brunch

I grew up on rice cereal and Cocoa Puffs, which didn't endear me to breakfast. As an adult I'd just grab a coffee and make it on fumes till lunchtime. But once I added a nourishing morning meal to my routine, I realized what a difference breakfast made in my day. So when a dietician told me that dry cereal is like giving your child a candy bar, I made a commitment to cook my kids a hot breakfast before school every day. The standard American breakfast is so tied to wheat, but with a little cauliflower creativity, you can enjoy amazing gluten-free alternatives to bagels (page 62), French Toast (page 76), and more, and you don't even have to give up cereal (page 68)!

everything bagels

MAKES 12 BAGELS

GLUTEN-FREE

GRAIN-FREE

PALEO

KETO FRIENDLY

VEGETARIAN

DAIRY-FREE

Growing up in small-town America, I'd never had a bagel until I got to college. To help pay my way through my studies, I worked at a breakfast place famous for its bagels, and I fell hard for them. After my diagnosis of lupus, I realized that bagels were giving me major inflammation—even more than bread—so bagels and I parted ways. Until cauliflower, like a knight in shining armor, brought bagel love back to my life. These little bagels don't taste exactly like bagels but are a fun inflammation-free alternative and light enough that you can eat more than one. They are best toasted and buttered or schmeared with cream cheese. To make rolls rather than bagels, don't make the hole. The everything spice is also delicious sprinkled over Avocado Toast (page 98) or pizza.

EVERYTHING SPICE MIX

2 teaspoons poppy seeds

2 teaspoons toasted sesame seeds

2 teaspoons dried garlic flakes

2 teaspoons dried onion flakes

1 teaspoon flaky sea salt

BAGELS

5½ cups (715 g) Cauliflower Rice (page 36)

2 large eggs, beaten

¼ cup (30 g) almond flour

¼ cup (35 g) tapioca flour

½ teaspoon garlic powder

½ teaspoon onion powder

1½ teaspoons sea salt

MAKE THE EVERYTHING SPICE MIX: Combine all the ingredients in a small bowl.

MAKE THE BAGELS: Preheat the oven to 400°F (205°C) and line a baking sheet with parchment paper.

Put the cauliflower rice in a large bowl. Add the eggs and stir to moisten it into a dough. In a small bowl, whisk together the almond flour, tapioca flour, garlic powder, onion powder, and salt. Add the almond flour mixture to the cauliflower mixture and stir until well combined.

Take a heaping ⅓ cup (2½ ounces/70 g to be precise) of the dough and put it in the palm of one hand. Cup your other hand and wrap your fingers around the dough and form it into a dome shape. Gently squeeze the dough to remove any excess liquid, then place the dough on the prepared baking sheet and flatten it slightly to form it into a bagel shape. Use your hands to smooth out any cracks. Press a hole through the center of each bagel with your finger. Repeat to form 12 bagels.

Sprinkle a scant ½ teaspoon of the spice mix over the top of each bagel and lightly press it in using your fingers.

Place the bagels in the oven and bake for about 30 minutes, until the bagels are set and lightly browned on the bottom. Remove from the oven and cool completely on the sheet. The bagels will keep covered in the refrigerator for up to 5 days or in the freezer for up to 1 month.

VARIATIONS

Egg Bagels: *Beat 1 teaspoon ground turmeric into 2 egg yolks and add to the dough. Top with the everything topping.*

Cinnamon-Raisin Bagels: *Omit the garlic powder and onion powder from the dough and add 2 teaspoons ground cinnamon, ¼ cup (35 g) currants or small raisins, and ¼ teaspoon grated orange zest to the dough. Skip the everything topping and dust the tops with extra cinnamon before placing the bagels in the oven.*

Sun-Dried Tomato Bagels: *Add ¼ cup (35 g) finely chopped oil-packed sun-dried tomatoes, 1 tablespoon paprika, and 1½ teaspoons dried basil to the dough. Add a big pinch of cayenne pepper for spice if you like. Top with the everything topping.*

blueberry pancakes

SERVES 4 (MAKES 8 PANCAKES)

GLUTEN-FREE
GRAIN-FREE
PALEO
KETO FRIENDLY
VEGAN
VEGETARIAN
DAIRY-FREE

Having white flour pancakes for breakfast is basically eating dessert for your first meal of the day. This recipe based on cauliflower rice is just as much of a treat but won't send you or your kids into sugar shock. The cauliflower rice gives the pancakes a slightly coarse texture reminiscent of stone-ground cornmeal and a blank slate to flavor with fruit. Use wild blueberries if you can find them for their diminutive size and high antioxidant content. For keto diets, finish with lots of ghee or butter and very lightly sprinkle with coconut sugar.

- 1 cup (130 g) Cauliflower Rice (page 36)
- ½ cup (60 g) almond flour
- ¼ cup (35 g) tapioca flour
- ½ teaspoon baking powder
- ¼ teaspoon sea salt
- 3 large eggs
- 1 tablespoon melted coconut oil, plus 4 teaspoons for the pan
- 3 tablespoons canned unsweetened coconut milk
- 1 tablespoon maple syrup (optional)
- ½ teaspoon pure vanilla extract
- ½ cup (80 g) fresh or frozen blueberries
- Grated zest of 1 lemon
- Topping suggestions: softened coconut butter, sliced fresh fruit, maple syrup, or coconut sugar, Berry Chia Jam (page 82), Almond Ricotta (page 58), toasted coconut

Put the cauliflower rice in a medium bowl. In a separate bowl, whisk together the almond meal, tapioca flour, baking powder, and salt. Add the dry ingredients to the cauliflower rice and stir to incorporate.

In another medium bowl, whisk the eggs, oil, coconut milk, maple syrup, if using, and vanilla. Add the egg mixture to the cauliflower rice mixture and stir until homogenous. Add the blueberries and lemon zest and stir gently to combine.

Heat a large skillet over medium heat. Add 1 teaspoon coconut oil, let it melt, and swirl it around. Cook two pancakes at a time, adding about ¼ cup (60 ml) batter for each, and, using the bottom of the measuring cup, spread the batter slightly so each pancake is about ¼ inch (6 mm) thick and 4 inches (10 cm) wide. Cook until bubbles form on the edges of the pancakes and they begin to set, about 1½ minutes, then use a metal spatula to flip the pancakes and cook on the second side for about 1 minute, until they are set and puff up slightly. Repeat with the remaining oil and batter to make 8 pancakes. Serve with your choice of toppings.

VARIATION

Berry Cinnamon Pancakes: *Substitute raspberries or blackberries for the blueberries and ½ teaspoon ground cinnamon for the lemon zest. Finish with a dusting of cinnamon.*

waffles

MAKES 6 WAFFLES

GLUTEN-FREE

GRAIN-FREE

PALEO

KETO

VEGETARIAN

My kids are huge waffle eaters. So Doug Smith, of our research and development team, and I experimented for months to come up with something they loved. Cauliflower meal, eggs, and cheese get these waffles to look and act like wheat waffles. They just need a couple of small tweaks: Be sure to grease the waffle maker really well, as otherwise the waffles will stick, and cook them two or three times longer than "regular" waffles in order to get them really brown. For keto diets, finish with lots of ghee or butter and very lightly sprinkle with coconut sugar. Note that the small amount of stevia isn't there to make the waffles sweet but to neutralize any residual cauliflower flavor.

7½ ounces (215 g/1½ cups loosely crumbled) Cauliflower Meal (page 20)

4 large eggs

½ cup (55 g) shredded low-moisture whole milk mozzarella cheese (not fresh)

½ cup (60 g) almond flour

2 tablespoons cream cheese

2 tablespoons avocado oil

5 drops unflavored liquid stevia

¼ teaspoon sea salt

3 teaspoons ghee

Topping suggestions: melted ghee or butter; sliced fresh fruit; maple syrup, honey, or coconut sugar; Berry Chia Jam (page 82); Almond Ricotta (page 58); toasted coconut

Preheat a waffle iron.

Combine all the ingredients except the ghee and toppings in a blender and blend until smooth, about 20 seconds, scraping the sides of the machine once if needed. Transfer to a bowl.

Make 6 waffles, brushing the waffle iron with ½ teaspoon ghee and using a scant ½ cup (120 ml) batter for each. Cook the waffles for about 7 minutes, until they are well browned. To remove the waffles from the iron, loosen the edges using a butter knife or fork, then slowly tuck the knife under the waffle to release it. Serve with your choice of toppings.

cinnamon apple porridge

SERVES 2

GLUTEN-FREE
GRAIN-FREE
PALEO

VEGAN
VEGETARIAN
DAIRY-FREE

As a little girl, I spent summers with my grandma Netta in La Grande, Oregon. She grew up in the Depression and knew how to make the most of any ingredient, which meant that rice cereal was a staple at her house. After my lupus diagnosis, I discovered that rice was an inflammation trigger, so I needed to get creative with my morning meal. My new version of rice cereal is not only low in calories and high in vitamins and minerals, but also decidedly *anti*-inflammatory. Multiple flavors and textures conceal this cereal's origins, and when you reach the bottom of the bowl you'll feel energized rather than weighed down by that heavy feeling oatmeal often leaves us with.

- 1¼ cups (360 ml) plain, unsweetened almond milk
- 2 tablespoons unsweetened almond butter
- 2 tablespoons maple syrup, plus more for serving (optional)
- 1 teaspoon ground cinnamon
- ½ teaspoon ground cardamom
- ⅛ teaspoon sea salt
- 2 cups (260 g) Cauliflower Rice (page 36)
- 1½ tablespoons currants
- 1 apple, coarsely shredded
- ⅛ teaspoon almond extract
- 1 tablespoon unsweetened coconut flakes
- 2 tablespoons chopped walnuts

Pour the almond milk into a small saucepan and whisk in the almond butter and maple syrup. Add the cinnamon, cardamom, and salt and whisk well. Add the cauliflower rice and currants, turn the heat to medium, and bring to a simmer. Reduce the heat to maintain a low simmer and cook, stirring often, until the cauliflower is softened but not mushy. Add the apple and almond extract and cook for about 1 minute, until the apple is slightly softened. Stir in the coconut. Spoon into bowls, top with walnuts and maple syrup, if using, and serve.

egg in a basket

SERVES 2

GLUTEN-FREE

GRAIN-FREE

KETO

Two of my favorite food groups—eggs and toast—unite in this take on the playful dish also known as toad in the hole or, more simply, egg in toast. Fancy it up by adding a handful of spinach along with the cheese or topping with salsa (pages 45–46) or pesto (pages 48–50). Watch carefully as you cook the crust and don't raise the heat higher than medium: The goal is for the crust to brown and the egg to set simultaneously. If you are using a frozen crust, stamp out the holes while it is slightly frozen to keep the crusts from tearing. Save the crust rounds for making crostini (page 96) or breadcrumbs (page 35).

1 Cali'flour Pizza Crust (page 26)

2 teaspoons ghee or unsalted butter

2 large eggs

Sea salt and freshly ground black pepper

¼ cup (30 g) shredded Cheddar or other melting cheese

2 strips bacon, cooked and crumbled (optional)

Sriracha or other hot sauce (optional)

Using a pizza wheel, cut the crust in half. Using a 3-inch (7.5-cm) cookie cutter or the top of a thin drinking glass, stamp out a hole from the middle of each crust half.

Melt the ghee in a 12-inch (30.5-cm) skillet that has a lid over medium heat (or cook the baskets one at a time in a smaller skillet). Using a metal spatula, carefully place the crusts in the skillet, then crack an egg directly into each hole and season with salt and pepper. Scatter the cheese on the exposed crust, cover the pan, and cook until the whites are set and the cheese is melted, about 3 minutes. Using the metal spatula, remove from the pan to plates and top with the bacon and hot sauce, if using.

SWAP

***To make this dish vegetarian:* Skip the bacon.**

chive and cheddar biscuits

MAKES 10 MUFFINS

GLUTEN-FREE

GRAIN-FREE

KETO

VEGETARIAN

Biscuits were a special treat for my grandma Netta when she was growing up during the Depression. When she could, she would make biscuits for any occasion: breakfast biscuits and gravy with saved bacon grease in a can, biscuits for lunch with some bologna and, yes, Miracle Whip, and biscuits with homemade butter with dinner. She never made a biscuit with cauliflower, but I think she would have loved these!

- 2 cups (260 g) Cauliflower Rice (page 36)
- 3 scallions (white and green parts), thinly sliced
- 2 tablespoons chopped fresh chives
- 4 teaspoons minced garlic
- 1 cup (115 g) shredded Cheddar cheese
- ¼ cup (25 g) grated Parmesan cheese
- 1 cup (115 g) almond flour
- ¼ cup (35 g) tapioca flour
- 1 teaspoon baking powder
- ¾ teaspoon sea salt
- ½ teaspoon freshly ground black pepper
- ½ cup (120 ml) canned unsweetened coconut milk
- 3 large eggs

Preheat the oven to 350°F (175°C). Line 10 holes of a muffin pan with parchment paper cups.

In a large bowl, combine the cauliflower rice, scallions, chives, garlic, ¾ cup (85 g) of the Cheddar, and the Parmesan. Mix to incorporate.

In a small bowl, whisk the almond flour, tapioca flour, baking powder, salt, and pepper. Add the almond flour mixture to the cauliflower rice mixture and mix thoroughly. Pour the coconut milk into a liquid measuring cup. Add the eggs and whisk to combine. Add the coconut milk mixture to the cauliflower mixture and stir, scraping the bottom, until the mixture is homogeneous.

Spoon the batter into the prepared muffin cups, filling them just about to the top. Sprinkle with the remaining ¼ cup (30 g) Cheddar cheese. Bake for 25 minutes, or until the biscuits are set but not colored (do not let them brown). Cool for 5 minutes in the pan, then remove from the pan and serve. The biscuits will keep, wrapped in plastic wrap, for up to 5 days in the refrigerator or up to 1 month in the freezer. Defrost at room temperature, then reheat in a toaster oven.

kale, scallion, and tomato egg muffins

SERVES 4

GLUTEN-FREE

GRAIN-FREE

PALEO

KETO FRIENDLY

VEGETARIAN

DAIRY-FREE

These egg muffins are set on a small circle of crust to give a pastry effect without adding gluten or excess carbs. The crust may rise slightly into the egg as it bakes, giving each muffin a unique appearance. You can enjoy these hot or at room temperature or make them in advance and reheat throughout the week. Lightly beat the eggs to prevent them from rising too much. If you are using a frozen crust, stamp out the holes while it's still slightly frozen to keep the crusts from tearing. Save the scraps for breadcrumbs (page 35).

- 1 Plant-Based Cali'flour Pizza Crust (page 28) or Paleo Cali'flour Pizza Crust (page 29)
- 6 large eggs
- ½ teaspoon sea salt
- ¼ teaspoon ground turmeric
- ¼ teaspoon freshly ground black pepper
- 8 small cherry tomatoes, quartered
- 3 tablespoons finely chopped kale (from 1 small leaf)
- ½ small scallion (green part only), very thinly sliced

Preheat the oven to 375°F (190°C). Line 8 holes of a muffin pan with paper cups.

Using a 2½-inch (6-cm) cookie cutter or the top of a drinking glass, cut out 8 circles from the crust. Press the crusts into the bottom and up the sides of the paper cups. If they tear, just press them together.

In a medium bowl, beat the eggs lightly, then beat in the salt, turmeric, and pepper. Put the tomatoes and kale in the bottom of the muffin cups, then pour the beaten egg into the cups and top with the scallion. Bake for 15 to 20 minutes, until the eggs are set. Cool in the pan for 2 minutes, then serve. Store leftovers in a covered container in the refrigerator for up to 4 days. Reheat in a toaster oven.

french toast

SERVES 2

GLUTEN-FREE

GRAIN-FREE

PALEO*

KETO FRIENDLY

VEGETARIAN

* If using ghee

My version of Sunday brunch won't leave you in carb overload. In fact, you can enjoy this French toast even if you're on a keto diet by being generous with the butter and finishing with a light sprinkle of coconut sugar. If there is egg left after dipping your bread, save it to make another round of French toast tomorrow.

2 large eggs, beaten

1 tablespoon unsweetened canned coconut milk or heavy cream

¼ teaspoon pure vanilla extract

¼ teaspoon ground cinnamon

Pinch of sea salt

4 slices New White Bread (page 30), well toasted

1 tablespoon ghee, butter, or coconut butter

Topping suggestions: melted ghee or butter; sliced fresh fruit; maple syrup, honey, or coconut sugar; Berry Chia Jam (page 82); Almond Ricotta (page 58); toasted coconut

Beat the eggs in a small bowl and whisk in the coconut milk, vanilla, cinnamon, and salt. Pour the egg mixture into a pie plate or shallow container. Dip the bread into the mixture and allow to soak for about 20 seconds on each side, then remove to a wire rack set on a plate and allow to sit for 1 to 2 minutes.

Melt the ghee in large skillet over medium heat. Add the bread and cook until golden brown, 2 to 3 minutes on each side. Place on plates and serve immediately with your choice of toppings.

SWAP

To make the French toast dairy-free: Make the bread without the ghee and use coconut oil for cooking.

VARIATION

Almond French Toast: *Swap almond extract for the vanilla and press sliced almonds into both sides of the bread after dipping it into the egg.*

huevos rancheros pizza

SERVES 4

GLUTEN-FREE

GRAIN-FREE

KETO FRIENDLY

VEGETARIAN

This gorgeous rendition of rancheros requires no deep-frying of tortillas but rather a simple bake of a Cali'flour pizza crust, a topping of salsa, and creamy avocado and cotija to melt into your mouth. Cotija cheese is a mild, salty firm cheese similar to feta. If unavailable, use feta. If your eggs attach to each other as you fry them, separate them with kitchen scissors then arrange them on the four corners of your crust. For added heat, make this pizza with a Spicy Jalapeño crust (page 26).

- 1 Cali'flour Pizza Crust (page 26)
- ¾ cup (180 ml) Green Salsa (page 46)
- 1 tablespoon ghee or extra-virgin olive oil
- 4 eggs (any size)
- Sea salt
- 2 tablespoons crumbled cotija or feta cheese
- ½ avocado, thinly sliced
- ½ small jalapeño chile (seeded if you like), thinly sliced
- 1 tablespoon torn fresh cilantro leaves
- ½ lime, cut into four wedges

Preheat the oven to 425°F (220°C). Line a baking sheet with parchment paper or get out your pizza pan and put the crust on it.

Spread ½ cup (120 ml) of the salsa over the crust. Place in the oven and bake for 8 to 10 minutes, until everything is hot.

Meanwhile, heat the ghee in a large skillet over medium-high heat. Crack in the eggs, sprinkle with salt, and cook for 5 minutes, or until the whites are set and the yolks are as runny or firm as you like them. Remove the eggs from the pan and set them on top of the crust. Dollop the remaining ¼ cup (60 ml) salsa over the pizza, avoiding the yolks, and top with the cheese. Arrange the avocado, chile, and cilantro on top. Slice and serve with lime wedges for squeezing.

SWAP

To make this pizza paleo: Use a Paleo crust (page 29) and substitute Almond Ricotta (page 58) for the cotija cheese.

VARIATION

Huevos Divorciados: *Use green salsa on half of the crust and Red Salsa (page 45) on the other.*

sandwiches and toasts

My father-in-law, Jim, was serious about his sandwiches. When my husband and I got married in New Orleans, we served muffaletta sandwiches as an appetizer in his honor. Jim will always be remembered for his place in so many of our big life events. He was a captain in the navy and a lover of his country and family—and, of course, a good sandwich! He passed away suddenly before I started Cali'flour Foods, but I think he would have approved of how I came up with a cauliflower pizza crust that doubles as sandwich bread. Recipes include a dairy-free, fermented take on cream cheese and jelly, variations on the cheese sandwich, crostini, and ten ways to serve avocado toast. If you are making your crusts from scratch, try forming them into squares rather than rounds.

cashew cream cheese and jam sandwich

SERVES 2 (MAKES 2 SANDWICHES)

GLUTEN-FREE

GRAIN-FREE

PALEO

VEGAN

VEGETARIAN

DAIRY-FREE

Tangy cashew cheese and crunchy jam made with chia seeds upgrades a classic sandwich for a new generation of plant-based kids and parents.

- 1 Plant-Based Cali'flour Pizza Crust (page 28)
- ¼ cup (55 g) Cashew Cream Cheese (page 59), at room temperature
- 3 tablespoons Berry Chia Jam (recipe follows)
- Extra-virgin olive oil or coconut oil cooking spray

Preheat a large cast-iron skillet over medium-high heat.

Using a pizza wheel or kitchen scissors, cut the crust in half, then cut each half in half again to make 4 triangles. Spread the cream cheese over half of the triangles and spread the jam on top. Top with the remaining triangles to complete the sandwiches.

Generously coat the skillet with cooking spray. Using a metal spatula, place the sandwiches in the skillet and cook for 2 minutes, or until browned on the bottom. Flip and cook for another 2 minutes, or until they are browned on the second side. Place on plates and serve.

berry chia jam

MAKES ABOUT ¾ CUP (180 ML)

GLUTEN-FREE

GRAIN-FREE PALEO

VEGAN VEGETARIAN

DAIRY-FREE

Little chia seeds are packed with heart-healthy omega-3 fatty acids and filled with fiber and protein. And because they absorb liquid like crazy, they add thickening power to jam just by stirring them in. If your jam isn't thick enough, add more chia seeds ½ teaspoon at a time, and if it's too thick, add a little water. Use any berry you like or a mix of seasonal fruit.

- 2 cups (about 8 ounces/225 g) fresh or frozen and thawed whole raspberries, blueberries, blackberries, or sliced strawberries
- 1 to 2 tablespoons maple syrup, to taste
- ¼ teaspoon pure vanilla extract
- ¼ teaspoon grated lemon zest (optional)
- 1 teaspoon fresh lemon juice (optional)
- 1½ tablespoons chia seeds

Put the berries and maple syrup in a small skillet and cook over medium heat, stirring frequently, until the berries begin to break down and become slightly syrupy, 5 to 7 minutes. Remove from the heat and mash the berries with the back of a wooden spoon or potato masher to make the jam as lumpy or smooth as you like. Add the vanilla and lemon zest and lemon juice, if using. Stir in the chia seeds and leave for 10 minutes for the seeds to swell and thicken the mixture. Transfer to a jar and cool completely. The jam will keep for up to 2 weeks in the refrigerator.

VARIATION

AB&J: *Sub almond butter for the cashew cream cheese.*

sweet potato, balsamic, and roasted red pepper sandwich

SERVES 2 (MAKES 2 SANDWICHES)

GLUTEN-FREE
GRAIN-FREE
PALEO

VEGAN
VEGETARIAN
DAIRY-FREE

While sweet potatoes aren't terribly low-carb, the bread in this sandwich is, so what normally would be a splurge becomes a guilt-free, nourishing lunch. Salt in a sandwich might seem superfluous, but don't skip it; it brings out the flavors of all the ingredients.

- 1 Plant-Based Cali'flour Pizza Crust (page 28)
- 3 tablespoons Roasted Garlic Cream (page 51; optional)
- ½ cup (165 g) mashed sweet potato
- 2 teaspoons balsamic vinegar
- ½ small roasted bell pepper, cut into thin strips
- Flaky sea salt and freshly ground black pepper
- Extra-virgin olive oil or coconut oil cooking spray
- Small handful of baby arugula or sprouts

Preheat a large cast-iron skillet over medium-high heat.

Using a pizza wheel or kitchen scissors, cut the crust in half, then cut each half in half again to make 4 triangles. Spread the garlic cream, if using, over half of the triangles, followed by the sweet potato. Sprinkle with the vinegar and top with roasted red pepper; season with salt and pepper. Place the remaining triangles on top to complete the sandwiches.

Generously coat the skillet with cooking spray. Using a metal spatula, place the sandwiches in the skillet and cook for 2 minutes, or until browned on the bottom. Flip and cook for another 2 minutes, or until they are browned on the second side. Tuck in the arugula leaves. Place on plates and serve.

VARIATION

Hummus, Balsamic, and Red Pepper: *Swap New Classic Hummus (page 152) for the sweet potato.*

almond ricotta and caramelized onion sandwich

SERVES 2 (MAKES 2 SANDWICHES)

GLUTEN-FREE

GRAIN-FREE

PALEO

KETO

VEGAN

VEGETARIAN

DAIRY-FREE

Sweet slow-cooked onions and tangy almond ricotta partner perfectly in this upscale vegan sandwich. This makes more caramelized onions than you'll need, so you'll have extra to make more sandwiches or freeze for later. If you are making the French Onion Soup (page 102), you could snag a few caramelized onions from the pot as a shortcut.

CARAMELIZED ONIONS

1 tablespoon extra-virgin olive oil

2 large yellow onions, thinly sliced

2 teaspoons balsamic vinegar

1 teaspoon chopped fresh thyme or rosemary

⅛ teaspoon sea salt

Pinch of freshly ground black pepper

SANDWICHES

1 Plant-Based Cali'flour Pizza Crust (page 28)

4 tablespoons (60 ml) Almond Ricotta (page 58)

4 small, thin tomato slices

Flaky sea salt and freshly ground black pepper

Olive oil or coconut oil cooking spray

Small handful of baby arugula or dandelion greens

MAKE THE CARAMELIZED ONIONS: Heat the oil in a large skillet over medium-high heat. Add the onions and cook, stirring often, until the onions start to brown and browned bits start to form on the bottom of the pan. Add 2 tablespoons water and scrape the pan. Continue to cook, stirring often, until browned bits form on the bottom of the pan again. Add another 2 tablespoons water and continue to cook, adding more water as needed, until the onions are completely softened and a rich dark brown, about 15 minutes total. Add the vinegar, thyme, salt, and pepper and cook for 3 minutes to incorporate the flavors. Remove from the pan and cool.

MAKE THE SANDWICHES: Preheat a large cast-iron skillet over medium-high heat.

Using a pizza wheel or kitchen scissors, cut the crust in half, then cut each half in half again to make 4 triangles. Spread 2 tablespoons almond ricotta each over two of the triangles and top each with 1 tablespoon caramelized onion and 2 tomato slices. Sprinkle with salt and pepper. Place the remaining triangles on top to complete the sandwiches.

Generously coat the skillet with cooking spray. Using a metal spatula, place the sandwiches in the skillet and cook for 2 minutes, or until browned on the bottom. Flip and cook for another 2 minutes, or until they are browned on the second side. Tuck in the arugula leaves. Place on plates and serve.

provolone, pesto, and tomato sandwich

SERVES 2 (MAKES 4 MINI SANDWICHES)

GLUTEN-FREE

GRAIN-FREE

KETO

VEGETARIAN

The only thing more comforting than a cheese sandwich is when you make yours on a cheese-containing crust! Follow the recipe as written, or use it as a blueprint for constructing a cheese sandwich using your personal favorites.

1 Cali'flour Pizza Crust (page 26)

4 teaspoons Cauliflower Leaf Pesto (page 48)

4 thin slices provolone cheese (1 ounce/28 g)

8 small, thin tomato slices

Preheat a medium cast-iron skillet over medium-high heat.

Using a pizza wheel or kitchen scissors, cut the crust in half, then cut each half into quarters to make 8 triangles. Spread 1 teaspoon pesto each over half of the triangles and top each with 1 slice cheese and 2 tomato slices. Place the remaining triangles on top to complete the sandwiches.

Using a metal spatula, place two of the sandwiches in the skillet and cook for about 1 minute, until browned on the bottom. Flip and cook for another 1 minute, or until they are browned on the second side and the cheese is melted. Repeat with the remaining two sandwiches, place on plates, and serve.

blt

SERVES 2 (MAKES 2 SANDWICHES)

GLUTEN-FREE

GRAIN-FREE

PALEO

KETO

DAIRY-FREE

Every bit as crave-worthy as the original. To make this sandwich even lower in carbs, use a Cali'flour Crust (page 26), skip the cooking spray, and decrease the cooking time to about 1 minute on each side.

1 Paleo Cali'flour Pizza Crust (page 29)

4 teaspoons mayonnaise

4 thin tomato slices

4 strips bacon, cooked

Flaky sea salt and freshly ground black pepper

4 small lettuce leaves

Olive oil or coconut oil cooking spray

Preheat a large cast-iron skillet over medium-high heat.

Spread the mayonnaise over the pizza crust. Using a pizza wheel or kitchen scissors, cut the crust in half, then cut each half in half again to make 4 triangles. Top two of the triangles with 2 tomato slices and 2 bacon strips each. Sprinkle with salt and pepper. Place the remaining triangles on top to complete the sandwiches.

Generously coat the skillet with cooking spray. Using a metal spatula, place the sandwiches in the skillet and cook for about 2 minutes, until browned on the bottom. Flip and cook for another 2 minutes, or until browned on the second side. Tuck in the lettuce leaves, place on plates, and serve.

prosciutto and monterey jack sandwich

SERVES 2 (MAKES 2 SANDWICHES)

GLUTEN-FREE

GRAIN-FREE

KETO FRIENDLY

An ideal grilled cheese sandwich is well browned on the outside and oozing with cheese on the inside. Ours goes a step further: When the crust hits the pan, the cheese it's made from melts into crispy bits to provide cheesy satisfaction inside and out! Any type of cheese and meat (or skip the meat) can be put into this sandwich equation. To add some heat, make your sandwich with pepper Jack cheese.

- 1 Cali'flour Pizza Crust (page 26)
- 1 teaspoon Dijon mustard
- 2 tablespoons grated Monterey Jack cheese
- 1½ ounces (40 g/3 slices) prosciutto, torn into pieces

Preheat a large cast-iron skillet over medium-high heat.

Using a pizza wheel or kitchen scissors, cut the crust in half, then cut each half in half again to make 4 triangles. Spread the mustard over half of the triangles, then top with the cheese and prosciutto.

Using a metal spatula, place the triangles in the skillet and cook for about 1 minute, until browned on the bottom. Place the remaining triangles on top to complete the sandwiches. Flip and cook for another 1 minute, or until they are browned on the second side and the cheese is melted. Place on plates and serve.

tahini turkey sandwiches

SERVES 2 (MAKES 2 SANDWICHES)

GLUTEN-FREE

GRAIN-FREE

PALEO

KETO FRIENDLY

DAIRY-FREE

Cucumber with a splash of vinegar adds a bright note to everyday turkey, and a spoonful of sauerkraut brings salty, tangy notes to the mix. A sour pickle would be a welcome sidekick. Instead of the tahini, you could use hummus.

- 1 Paleo Cali'flour Pizza Crust (page 29)
- ¼ cup (60 ml) Creamy Tahini Sauce (page 52)
- 6 to 8 thin slices cucumber
- 1 teaspoon apple cider vinegar
- Flaky sea salt and coarsely ground black pepper
- 2 teaspoons chopped fresh flat-leaf parsley or thyme
- 1 ounce (28 g) thinly sliced deli turkey
- Extra-virgin olive oil or coconut oil cooking spray
- 1 tablespoon sauerkraut (optional)

Preheat a large cast-iron skillet over medium-high heat.

Using a pizza wheel or kitchen scissors, cut the crust in half, then cut each half in half again to make 4 triangles. Spread the tahini sauce over each of the triangles. Top half of the triangles with the cucumber, vinegar, a pinch of salt and pepper, the parsley, and turkey. Place the remaining triangles on top to complete the sandwiches.

Generously coat the skillet with cooking spray. Using a metal spatula, place the sandwiches in the skillet and cook for 2 minutes, or until browned on the bottom. Flip and cook for another 2 minutes, or until they are browned on the second side. Tuck in the sauerkraut, if using. Place on plates and serve.

VARIATION

Tahini Ham Sandwich: *Sub ham for the turkey.*

crostini two ways

EACH SERVES 4 (MAKES 8 CROSTINI EACH)

GLUTEN-FREE

GRAIN-FREE

KETO FRIENDLY

VEGETARIAN

Earthy, tangy, sweet, and salty, these crostini have it all (plus cauliflower!). You can sub in a cauliflower crust for the baguette in any crostini recipe, keeping your toppings on the lighter side. Save the scraps from cutting out your crumbs for breadcrumbs (page 35)

1 Cali'flour Pizza Crust (page 26)

Preheat the oven to 425°F (220°C) and line a baking sheet with parchment paper.

Use a 2½- to 3-inch (6- to 7.5-cm) cookie cutter or the top of a drinking glass to cut out 8 rounds of crust. Place on the prepared baking sheet and bake, turning once, until they are crispy and well browned, 7 to 10 minutes. Remove from the oven and cool.

beet, goat cheese, and salty pistachio crostini

1 roasted red beet (see page 172), cut into small cubes

¾ teaspoon balsamic vinegar, or to taste

Sea salt and freshly ground black pepper

8 teaspoons soft goat cheese, at room temperature

1½ teaspoons finely chopped shelled salted toasted pistachios

In a medium bowl, toss the beet with the vinegar and season with salt and pepper. Spread the goat cheese over the rounds and top with the beets. Sprinkle the pistachios on top and finish with a grinding of the peppermill. Serve immediately.

shredded brussels sprouts and brie crostini

¼ teaspoon grated lemon zest

1 teaspoon fresh lemon juice

1 teaspoon extra-virgin olive oil

½ teaspoon honey

⅛ teaspoon sea salt

Pinch of smoked paprika

5 medium Brussels sprouts, shredded on the large holes of a box grater

2 ounces (55 g) Brie cheese, softened, cut into 8 wedges

Drizzle of truffle oil (optional)

1 teaspoon toasted pine nuts

Preheat the broiler.

In a small bowl, whisk together the lemon zest, lemon juice, olive oil, honey, salt, and smoked paprika. Add the Brussels sprouts and toss to coat. Place a wedge of Brie on each round and top with the Brussels sprouts. Place under the broiler and broil for 2 to 3 minutes, until the cheese is melted. Remove from the broiler and finish with a tiny drizzle of truffle oil, if using, and the pine nuts. Serve immediately.

avocado toast ten ways

SERVES 3

GLUTEN-FREE

GRAIN-FREE

KETO FRIENDLY

VEGETARIAN

My home state of California is Avocado Toast Central Headquarters, with mom-and-pop shops and fine-dining establishments alike boasting their version of avocado spread on a piece of bread. In true California spirit, I have my own takes on avocado toast. These are some of my favorites.

- 1 Cali'flour Pizza Crust (page 26)
- 1 large ripe avocado
- 1 teaspoon fresh lime or lemon juice, or to taste
- Flaky sea salt and freshly ground black pepper

Preheat the oven to 425°F (220°C) and line a baking sheet with parchment paper.

Using a pizza wheel or kitchen scissors, cut the crust in half, then cut each half in thirds to make 6 triangles. Place on the prepared baking sheet and bake until they are crispy and well browned, 8 to 10 minutes. Remove from the oven and cool.

Cut the avocado in half and remove the pit. Scoop out the avocado flesh and put it in a bowl. Add the lime juice and mash with a fork until it is as smooth or lumpy as you like. Season with salt and pepper. Spread on the crust, add your choice of toppings, and serve.

VARIATIONS

Caprese: *Top with halved small cherry tomatoes and torn fresh basil leaves; finish with a drizzle of balsamic vinegar.*

Cucumber: *Spread the toast with Cashew Cream Cheese (page 59) or dairy cream cheese. Top with sliced cucumber, a drizzle of apple cider vinegar, and a pinch of red pepper flakes.*

Radish: *Top with thin slices of watermelon radish or other radish, black sesame seeds, and flaky salt.*

Salsa: *Top with Red Salsa (page 45) or Green Salsa (page 46) and torn cilantro leaves.*

Pesto: *Mix pesto (page 48 or 50) into the avocado. Top with pumpkin seeds or pine nuts and coarsely ground black pepper.*

Garlic: *Mix Roasted Garlic Cream (page 51) into the avocado. Top with dried garlic flakes and coarsely ground black pepper.*

Tahini: *Drizzle Creamy Tahini Sauce (page 52) over the toast and sprinkle with thinly sliced scallion and sesame seeds.*

Ricotta: *Finish with Almond Ricotta (page 58) or dairy ricotta, a sprinkle of grated lemon zest, and coarsely ground black pepper.*

White Bean: *Add White Bean Spread (page 54) before the avocado. Finish with a sprinkle of thyme leaves and coarsely ground black pepper.*

Everything: *Top with Everything Spice (page 62).*

soups and salads

Cauliflower makes a creamy soup base that takes on the flavors you add to it. And with a Cali'flour pizza crust as your crouton, French onion soup becomes a reality for gluten-free folks. I've included some of my favorite salad pizzas here, including Caesar and roasted orange and radicchio, but really any veggies over hummus will impress your guests. Think of a pizza crust as a salad delivery system!

french onion soup

SERVES 6

GLUTEN-FREE

GRAIN-FREE

KETO FRIENDLY

French onion soup is a dish I had to give up after being diagnosed with an autoimmune disease and having to remove gluten from my diet. But now, with a little creative crafting of a Cali'flour pizza crust, my favorite soup with that cheesy bread is back in my life! Low and slow caramelization of the onions is the key to a great French onion soup. No special skill is required, but it does take a good hour, so consider cranking up some tunes and multitasking by tackling another dish or dessert in between stirs.

- 2 pounds (910 g) medium yellow or red onions, or a mixture
- 4 tablespoons (½ stick/55 g) unsalted butter
- 3 cloves garlic, minced
- ½ cup (120 ml) dry sherry
- 2 quarts (2 L) beef or chicken stock
- 2 sprigs thyme, plus thyme leaves for garnish
- 1 bay leaf
- 1 teaspoon sea salt, or to taste
- 1½ teaspoons sherry vinegar, or to taste
- 1 teaspoon coconut aminos
- Freshly ground black pepper
- 1 Cali'flour Pizza Crust (page 26)
- 2 tablespoons Dijon or grainy mustard (optional)
- 5 ounces (140 g) Gruyère cheese, grated

Cut the onions in half through the root end, then quarter them.

In a large saucepan, melt the butter over medium heat. Add the onions and cook for about 10 minutes, until they are starting to soften. Lower the heat to medium-low and cook, stirring often, until the onions are well browned but still hold their shape, about 1 hour. Add the garlic and cook for 5 minutes, or until it is softened.

Increase the heat to medium-high, add the sherry, and cook, stirring to release any browned bits from the pan, until it is reduced, about 5 minutes. Add the stock, thyme, bay leaf, and salt and bring to a simmer. Cover, reduce the heat to maintain a simmer, and cook for 45 minutes to combine the flavors. Remove from the heat, add the vinegar and coconut aminos, and season with pepper. Taste and add more salt, vinegar, and/or pepper as needed.

While the soup is finishing up, preheat the oven to 375°F. Line a baking sheet with parchment paper or get out your pizza pan and put your crust on it.

Bake for about 5 minutes, until the crust starts to crisp. Remove from the oven and increase the oven temperature to 450°F.

Spread the mustard, if using, over the crust and top with the cheese. Return to the oven and bake for another 5 to 10 minutes, until the cheese is melted and the crust is crisp. Transfer to a cutting board and use a pizza wheel to cut approximately 1-inch (2.5-cm) strips across, then cut in the opposite direction to make square or rectangular crouton shapes.

Ladle the soup into bowls. Top with the croutons, sprinkle with thyme and some black pepper, and serve.

cream of tomato soup

SERVES 4

GLUTEN-FREE

GRAIN-FREE

KETO FRIENDLY

VEGETARIAN*

* If made with vegetable stock

My youngest son, Grant, is a soup lover. Soup for fall, soup for winter, and even soup for summer. Pair this bowl of creamy tomato bliss with a grilled cheese sandwich (page 92), and my little reptile-loving comedian is one happy boy!

1 tablespoon extra-virgin olive oil, plus more for drizzling

1 onion, chopped

2 cloves garlic, minced

1 teaspoon dried Italian seasoning

1 tablespoon tomato paste

1 (28-ounce/794-g) can diced tomatoes, with juices

2 cups (480 ml) vegetable or chicken stock

2 cups (214 g) chopped cauliflower florets and stems

½ teaspoon sea salt

½ teaspoon freshly ground black pepper

¼ cup (60 ml) heavy cream or coconut cream

¼ cup (10 g) small fresh basil leaves

2 tablespoons Cali'flour Breadcrumbs (using a Cali'flour Pizza Crust; page 35), or ½ cup (15 g) Croutons (page 33)

Red pepper flakes (optional)

Heat the oil in a large saucepan over medium heat. Add the onion and cook until softened, about 5 minutes. Add the garlic and cook for 1 minute. Add the Italian seasoning and cook for 30 seconds. Stir in the tomato paste. Add the tomatoes and their juices, then add the stock, cauliflower, salt, and pepper and bring to a simmer. Reduce the heat to maintain a simmer, cover, and cook, stirring occasionally, for 20 minutes, or until the cauliflower is soft.

Working in two batches, transfer the soup to a blender (be careful blending hot liquids) and blend until smooth. Rinse out the pan and return the soup to the pan. Add the cream and bring to a simmer. Spoon into bowls and top with the basil, breadcrumbs, a sprinkle of red pepper flakes, if using, and a drizzle of oil.

SWAPS

To make this soup paleo: Use coconut cream and a Paleo crust (page 29). To make it vegan, use coconut cream, vegetable stock, and a Plant-Based crust (page 28).

creamy cauliflower soup

SERVES 6

GLUTEN-FREE

GRAIN-FREE

PALEO*

KETO FRIENDLY

VEGAN†

VEGETARIAN†

DAIRY-FREE

* If omitting sherry

† If made with vegetable stock

This creamy yet ethereally light soup makes use of the cauliflower florets, stems, and core so nothing goes to waste. Anise notes from the fennel ground the soup, and a small amount of saffron adds a golden hue, floral flavor, and otherworldly aroma. Pure heaven!

- ⅛ teaspoon saffron
- 2 tablespoons extra-virgin olive oil, plus more for drizzling
- 1 onion, chopped
- 1 bulb fennel, cored and sliced, fronds chopped
- 2 tablespoons dry sherry (optional)
- 1 small head cauliflower, florets and stems cut into bite-size pieces, core thinly sliced
- 2 cups (480 ml) vegetable or chicken stock
- 1 cup (240 ml) canned unsweetened coconut milk
- ¾ teaspoon sea salt, or to taste
- ½ teaspoon freshly ground white pepper, plus more for finishing
- 2 teaspoons fresh lemon juice, or to taste

Put the saffron in a tiny bowl or ramekin. Add 2 teaspoons hot water and leave to steep for 20 minutes.

Heat the oil in a large saucepan over medium heat. Add the onion and fennel and cook until softened, 5 to 7 minutes. Add the sherry, if using, and cook until it evaporates, about 30 seconds. Add the cauliflower, stock, coconut milk, salt, white pepper, and bloomed saffron and bring to a simmer. Reduce the heat to maintain a low simmer, cover, and cook until the cauliflower is softened, about 15 minutes.

Working in two batches, transfer the soup to a blender (be careful blending hot liquids) and blend on high speed until very smooth, about 2 minutes. Rinse out the pan and return the soup to the pan. Add the lemon juice. Taste and add more salt and/or lemon juice if needed and add a little water or stock if the soup is too thick. Spoon into bowls, sprinkle with fennel fronds, add a drizzle of oil, and finish with a grind of the pepper mill.

VARIATION

Truffle Creamy Cauliflower Soup: *Omit the saffron and finish the soup with a splash of truffle oil.*

hummus and mediterranean salad pizza

SERVES 3

GLUTEN-FREE
GRAIN-FREE
PALEO
KETO
VEGAN
VEGETARIAN
DAIRY-FREE

If you're looking for a base for your plant-based pizzas, you won't go wrong with hummus. The hummus itself contains cauliflower, and this salad shines with salty, bold, and sweet flavors. Tip: Any greens your crisper drawer contains will make a great hummus topper.

- 1 Plant-Based Cali'flour Pizza Crust (page 28), baked for a few minutes longer than specified in the recipe
- ⅓ cup (75 ml) New Classic Hummus (page 152)
- ¼ cup (25 g) thinly sliced cucumber
- ½ roasted red bell pepper, cut into thin strips
- 2 olive oil–marinated artichoke hearts, quartered
- 2 or 3 black olives, pitted and sliced
- 3 fresh flat-leaf parsley leaves, torn
- 1 teaspoon extra-virgin olive oil
- ½ teaspoon balsamic vinegar
- Pinch of flaky sea salt and freshly ground black pepper

Spread the hummus over the crust. Arrange the cucumber, roasted pepper, artichoke hearts, olives, and parsley over the crust. Drizzle the oil and vinegar over the top and finish with the salt and black pepper. Slice and serve.

caesar salad pizza

SERVES 3, WITH EXTRA CAESAR DRESSING

GLUTEN-FREE

GRAIN-FREE

KETO FRIENDLY

Caesar was a gateway salad for me. It was the first form of greens I would eat, and now it's a staple for my entire family. If we are out to dinner, you can bet both my husband, Jim, and my daughter, Caroline, will order a Caesar salad. This is a pizza dedicated to the father and daughter who are so much alike. This recipe makes more dressing than you'll need; leftover dressing will keep in the fridge for up to three days.

CAESAR DRESSING (MAKES ABOUT ¾ CUP/180 ML)

- 1 large clove garlic, pressed through a garlic press
- 2 tablespoons fresh lemon juice, or to taste
- 2 large egg yolks
- 4 tinned anchovy fillets
- 1 teaspoon Worcestershire sauce
- ¼ cup (25 g) finely grated Parmesan cheese
- ½ cup (240 ml) avocado oil
- ¼ teaspoon freshly ground black pepper

PIZZA

- 1 Cali'flour Pizza Crust (page 26), baked for a few minutes longer than specified in the recipe
- 1½ cups (85 g) shredded, sliced, or torn romaine hearts
- ¼ cup (8 g) Croutons (page 33)
- 1 tablespoon grated Parmesan cheese
- Red pepper flakes (optional)

MAKE THE CAESAR DRESSING: In a mini food processor, combine the garlic and lemon juice and let sit for 10 minutes. Add the egg yolks, anchovies, Worcestershire sauce, and cheese and pulse to combine and mince the anchovies. Transfer to a medium bowl. Whisking constantly, slowly drizzle in the oil, then whisk in the pepper. Taste and add more pepper and/or lemon juice if needed.

MAKE THE PIZZA: Spread 1 tablespoon of the dressing over the pizza crust. Toss the lettuce with 2 tablespoons dressing. Arrange the salad over the pizza, drizzle with 1 tablespoon dressing, and top with the croutons. Finish with the cheese and some red pepper flakes, if using, then slice and serve.

VARIATIONS

Chicken Caesar Pizza: *Add ¼ cup (50 g) shredded cooked chicken.*

Sea Caesar Pizza: *Add a generous garnish of dulse seaweed flakes.*

Kale Caesar Pizza: *Sub kale for the lettuce.*

roasted orange and radicchio salad pizza

SERVES 3

GLUTEN-FREE

GRAIN-FREE

KETO FRIENDLY

VEGETARIAN

Roasting oranges is a revelation. As they spend some time in the oven, their sweetness concentrates, their orange flavor intensifies, and they beckon you to make more and more! You could roast the small amount of oranges called for in this recipe in a toaster oven, or cook up an extra two or three for more pizzas or to serve drizzled with honey for dessert.

Extra-virgin olive oil cooking spray

1 small orange

2 ounces (55 g) soft goat cheese, at room temperature

2 tablespoons heavy cream

1 Cali'flour Pizza Crust (page 26), baked for a few minutes longer than specified in the recipe

¼ cup (10 g) thinly sliced radicchio

Drizzle of balsamic vinegar

Preheat the oven to 425°F (220°C). Coat a small baking sheet or ovenproof skillet with cooking spray.

Using a paring knife, remove the peel and white pith from the orange, then slice it ¼ inch (6 mm) thick (a serrated knife works well), reserving the small ends for later. Place the orange slices on the prepared sheet and roast for 15 to 20 minutes, until softened and blackened in spots.

Put the goat cheese in a small bowl. Add the cream and whisk with a fork to incorporate. Spread the goat cheese over the crust. Set the roasted orange slices on the crust and arrange slices of radicchio between the orange slices. Finish with a squeeze of the reserved orange ends and the vinegar, then slice and serve.

SWAP

To make this pizza vegan: Use a Plant-Based crust (page 28) and replace the goat cheese and heavy cream with a mix of Cashew Cream Cheese (page 59) and coconut cream.

fig, goat cheese, and arugula salad pizza

SERVES 3

GLUTEN-FREE

GRAIN-FREE

KETO FRIENDLY

VEGETARIAN

Figs feel right at home in both sweet and savory preparations. Creamy fresh goat cheese, peppery arugula, and a drizzle of balsamic meet with them to make this one of my favorite salad pizzas.

- 2 ounces (55 g) soft goat cheese, at room temperature
- 2 tablespoons heavy cream
- 1 Cali'flour Pizza Crust (page 26), baked for a few minutes longer than specified in the recipe
- 2 large fresh or dried figs, sliced
- 1 cup (20 g) lightly packed arugula
- Drizzle of balsamic vinegar

Put the goat cheese in a small bowl. Add the cream and whisk with a fork to incorporate.

Spread the goat cheese over the crust. Arrange the figs over the cheese, top with the arugula, and finish with the vinegar.

VARIATION

Beet, Goat Cheese, and Arugula Salad Pizza: *Trade ¼ cup (45 g) diced roasted beets (see page 172) for the figs.*

italian bread salad

SERVES 2

GLUTEN-FREE

GRAIN-FREE

PALEO*

KETO FRIENDLY

VEGETARIAN

* If making the bread with ghee

The base of traditional bread salad, or *panzanella*, is stale or toasted crusty bread tossed with tomatoes and an herb dressing and left for a bit to soak up the juices. I recently spent some time in Italy for research and development with my COO, Jimi Sturgeon-Smith, and Doug Smith of our research and development team. You could say that we ate our way through Italy, and this recipe is inspired by our time there. As we use a soft bread in this version, you can bypass the soaking step. Juicy, ripe tomatoes make this dish, so hold out for the season and seek out beautiful heirloom tomatoes of varying colors. Feel free to add other vegetables such as sliced cucumber or bell pepper.

1 pound (455 g) juicy ripe tomatoes, cored and cut into bite-size pieces

¼ teaspoon sea salt, plus more as needed

1 tablespoon red wine vinegar

½ teaspoon Dijon mustard

1 clove garlic, pressed through a garlic press

⅛ teaspoon freshly ground black pepper, or to taste

2 tablespoons extra-virgin olive oil

3 slices New White Bread (page 30), cut into ½-inch (12-mm) cubes and toasted well

¼ small red onion, thinly sliced

¼ cup (10 g) lightly packed fresh basil leaves, torn

¼ cup (10 g) lightly packed fresh mint leaves, torn

Put the tomatoes in a strainer set over a bowl. Add the salt and toss. Set aside at room temperature to drain, tossing a few times, for 15 to 30 minutes. Remove the strainer from the bowl and whisk the vinegar, mustard, garlic, and pepper into the bowl with the tomato juice. Whisk in the oil. Add the tomatoes, bread, onion, basil, and mint to the dressing and toss to coat. Taste and add more salt and pepper if needed.

lemony fennel cauliflower salad

SERVES 4 TO 6

GLUTEN-FREE

GRAIN-FREE

PALEO

KETO FRIENDLY

VEGAN*

VEGETARIAN

DAIRY-FREE

* If using maple syrup

Crunchy, perky, and a little sweet, this raw cauliflower salad is a taste and texture sensation. Lemon in three forms—juice, zest, and preserved lemon—brings the salad together with a punch of salty, sour, floral deliciousness. Preserved lemons, which are lemons pickled in salt, are a condiment used frequently in North African cuisine. Their flavor is simultaneously mellow and intensely lemony, transforming any salad you add them to. Preserved lemons can be found in specialty grocers or online. Rinse them of excess salt before using. If unavailable, skip them and double up on the lemon zest.

¼ cup (35 g) currants

1 small head cauliflower

1 small bulb fennel, cored and very thinly sliced, fronds chopped

½ preserved lemon, finely chopped

¼ cup (30 g) roasted salted shelled pistachios, chopped

¼ cup (60 ml) fresh lemon juice

2 teaspoons honey or maple syrup

1¼ teaspoons flaky sea salt, or to taste

½ teaspoon freshly ground black pepper

3 tablespoons extra-virgin olive oil

½ cup (25 g) chopped fresh flat-leaf parsley

½ cup (25 g) chopped fresh mint

Soak the currants in hot water to cover for 20 minutes while you prep your ingredients. Drain before using.

Trim the cauliflower of its leaves and finely chop the leaves. Cut the core from the cauliflower, then cut the cauliflower and stem into large pieces. Working in two batches, put the cauliflower florets and stem pieces in a food processor and pulse until broken down into chickpea-size pieces. Place in a bowl along with the cauliflower leaves and add the sliced fennel, preserved lemon, pistachios, and currants.

In a small bowl, whisk together the lemon juice, honey, salt, and pepper, then slowly whisk in the oil until emulsified. Add to the cauliflower mixture and toss to fully coat. Add the parsley, mint, and ¼ cup (13 g) chopped fennel fronds. Leave for at least 1 hour to marinate, then spoon into bowls and serve.

cauliflower rice

Just about anything you can do with regular rice, you can do with cauliflower rice, with fewer calories and bonus cruciferous nutrition. This chapter, dedicated to the new white rice, includes adaptations of classics from egg fried rice, burrito bowls, sushi rolls, and a take on mashed potatoes for the low-carb generation. To save time, you can start with store-bought cauliflower rice. You'll find it in the produce aisle of your grocery store.

kimchi, bacon, and egg fried cauliflower rice

SERVES 4

GLUTEN-FREE

GRAIN-FREE

PALEO

KETO FRIENDLY

DAIRY-FREE

When I was growing up, my mom would often whip up fried rice with an egg in it to feed us a quick meal, but for my kids, I make it egg fried cauliflower rice so they are getting maximum nutrition from their meal. Even my oldest son, James, who doesn't like vegetables, will go for cauliflower fried rice. He takes his without the kimchi, but for all you adults out there, the mix of pungent kimchi and salty, fatty bacon is not to be missed!

- 4 strips bacon
- 3 large eggs
- ¼ teaspoon ground turmeric
- ¼ teaspoon sea salt, plus a pinch for the cauliflower rice
- ¼ teaspoon freshly ground black pepper
- 5 cups (650 g) Cauliflower Rice (page 36)
- 2 cloves garlic, pressed through a garlic press
- 1 tablespoon extra-virgin olive oil or reserved bacon fat
- 3 tablespoons coconut aminos
- 1 teaspoon toasted sesame oil
- 1 cup (150 g) chopped kimchi, plus more for serving
- 2 tablespoons kimchi juice from the jar
- 2 scallions (white and green parts), thinly sliced
- 2 teaspoons tan or black sesame seeds

Cook the bacon in a large skillet over medium-high heat until crisp, about 5 minutes. Remove the bacon to a paper towel–lined plate, let cool, and crumble. Drain off all but 1 tablespoon fat from the pan (reserve the drained-off fat in a small heatproof cup, if you'd like) and reduce the heat to medium.

Beat the eggs in a medium bowl, then beat in the turmeric, ¼ teaspoon salt, and the pepper. Add the eggs to the pan you cooked the bacon in and tilt the skillet so the egg forms a flat layer. Cook without stirring for about 2 minutes, until the egg is firm on the bottom and mostly cooked through. Slide a large spatula under the egg, flip, and cook on the second side until fully cooked, about 1 minute more. Remove to a cutting board and cut into ribbons.

Heat the cauliflower rice, garlic, and a pinch of salt in a medium saucepan over medium-high heat, stirring often, for 3 to 5 minutes to remove excess moisture. Add the olive oil and cook for 1 minute, then add the coconut aminos and sesame oil. Remove from the heat and add the kimchi and kimchi juice.

Spoon the kimchi cauliflower rice into bowls; top with the egg ribbons, bacon, scallions, and sesame seeds; and serve.

SWAP

To make this rice bowl vegan: Use vegan kimchi and omit the bacon and egg.

VARIATION

Simple Egg Fried Rice: *Omit the kimchi and kimchi juice and add cooked vegetables of your choice.*

shrimp and cauliflower leaf grits

SERVES 4

GLUTEN-FREE

GRAIN-FREE

KETO FRIENDLY

For eight years, my husband, Jim, and I lived in New Orleans, where we ate our fair share of shrimp and grits. This cauliflower rice take on the classic is even easier to make and adds cauliflower leaves to the mix for their incredible flavor. If you don't have cauliflower leaves on hand, you can substitute bok choy.

6 cups (780 g) Cauliflower Rice (page 36)

2 cloves garlic, pressed through a garlic press

½ cup (120 ml) chicken stock

¾ teaspoon sea salt, or to taste

½ teaspoon coarsely ground black pepper, plus more for topping

¼ cup (60 ml) heavy cream

2 tablespoons unsalted butter

½ cup (55 g) shredded Cheddar cheese

¼ cup (25 g) grated Parmesan cheese, plus more for topping

1 pound (455 g) large shrimp, peeled and deveined

1 tablespoon extra-virgin olive oil

1 cup (70 g) thinly sliced cauliflower leaves

½ teaspoon grated lemon zest

2 teaspoons fresh lemon juice, or to taste

1 tablespoon chopped fresh flat-leaf parsley

Heat the cauliflower rice and garlic in a medium saucepan over medium-high heat, stirring often, for 3 to 5 minutes to remove excess moisture from the cauliflower. Add the stock, ½ teaspoon of the salt, and the pepper, bring to a simmer, and cook for 3 minutes, or until the liquid is mostly absorbed and the cauliflower rice is slightly softened but still al dente. Stir in the cream and butter until the butter is melted. Stir in the Cheddar and Parmesan cheeses until melted. Remove from the heat.

Rinse the shrimp and pat dry with paper towels. Season with the remaining ¼ teaspoon salt. In a large skillet, heat the oil over medium-high heat. Add the shrimp one by one in clockwise order around the edge of the pan without touching and cook without stirring until the shrimp start to turn pink, about 2 minutes. Using tongs, turn the shrimp in the order you placed them in the pan and cook until the second side turns pink and the shrimp are just about cooked through, about another 2 minutes. Move the shrimp to one side of the pan, add the cauliflower leaves, and cook for about 30 seconds to start to wilt them, then stir the leaves into the shrimp until fully wilted and the shrimp is cooked through. Remove from the heat and add the lemon zest and juice.

Spoon the cauliflower rice into bowls and serve topped with the shrimp. Finish with a squeeze of lemon juice, a sprinkle of Parmesan cheese, and the parsley and serve.

spicy mayo and grapefruit tuna poke bowl

SERVES 2

GLUTEN-FREE
GRAIN-FREE
PALEO
KETO
DAIRY-FREE

I'm a tuna-holic. And I love anything with raw fish in it, from sushi to ceviche and bowls filled with rice and fish, like this tuna poke updated with cauliflower rice. A very light dressing adds toasty, citrusy notes to the tuna while highlighting the freshness of the fish, and a spicy mayo adds creamy deliciousness. Togarashi is a Japanese spice powder based on sesame seeds, orange peel, and chiles and can be found in Asian markets. If unavailable, you can use a mild chile powder or omit it.

SPICY MAYO

¼ cup (60 ml) mayonnaise

1 tablespoon hot sauce

CAULIFLOWER RICE

2 cups (260 g) Cauliflower Rice (page 36)

2 teaspoons extra-virgin olive oil

⅛ teaspoon sea salt

TUNA

1 tablespoon coconut aminos

1 teaspoon toasted sesame oil

½ teaspoon honey

½ teaspoon grated grapefruit zest

Pinch of sea salt

8 ounces (225 g) raw sashimi-grade tuna, cut into ½-inch (12-mm) cubes

1 scallion (white and green parts), thinly sliced

1 teaspoon tan or black sesame seeds

FOR SERVING

1 small avocado, thinly sliced

4 grapefruit segments, chopped

1 large radish, cut into matchsticks

2 tablespoons fresh grapefruit juice

Flaky sea salt

½ sheet nori seaweed, cut into thin strips with scissors

Sprinkle of togarashi or chile powder (optional)

MAKE THE SPICY MAYO: In a small bowl, whisk the mayonnaise and hot sauce together.

MAKE THE CAULIFLOWER RICE: Heat the cauliflower rice in a medium skillet over medium-high heat, stirring often, for 3 to 5 minutes to remove excess moisture. Add the oil and salt and cook for 1 minute more.

MAKE THE TUNA: In a medium bowl, whisk the coconut aminos, sesame oil, honey, grapefruit zest, and salt. Add the tuna, scallion, and sesame seeds and stir to coat. Let sit for 5 minutes.

TO SERVE: Divide the cauliflower rice between two bowls. Arrange the tuna, avocado, grapefruit segments, and radish over the cauliflower rice. Drizzle the grapefruit juice on top and add a pinch of flaky salt. Finish with the spicy mayo, nori, and togarashi powder, if using, and serve immediately.

cream cheese salmon sushi rolls

SERVES 2 OR 3 (MAKES 6 ROLLS)

GLUTEN-FREE

GRAIN-FREE

KETO FRIENDLY

My husband, Jim, and I share a great love for sushi, and we have a family tradition of rolling up a bunch before the presidential debates every four years. Sitting back with a plate full of fish wrapped in seaweed and dipped into spicy mayo is a great way of getting through those particularly tough election seasons. I mix a little cream cheese into cauliflower rice to create the slightly sticky effect of sushi rice. If you don't have a sushi mat, don't worry: you can still make a good roll without one.

CAULIFLOWER RICE

3 cups (390 g) Cauliflower Rice (page 36)

2 teaspoons apple cider vinegar

¼ teaspoon sea salt

¼ cup (55 g) cream cheese, softened

ROLLS

½ medium cucumber

4 ounces (115 g) skinless sashimi-grade salmon

3 sheets nori seaweed

FOR SERVING

Coconut aminos

Spicy Mayo (page 126; optional)

Pickled ginger (optional)

Wasabi (optional)

MAKE THE CAULIFLOWER RICE: Heat the cauliflower rice in a large skillet over medium-high heat, stirring often, for 5 minutes to remove excess moisture. Remove from the heat and stir in the vinegar and salt. Add the cream cheese and stir until fully incorporated. Remove to a plate to cool completely.

MAKE THE ROLLS: Peel the cucumber, cut it in half lengthwise, and scoop out the seeds. Cut the cucumber into ¼-inch-wide (6-mm) strips. Cut the salmon into ½-inch-wide (12-mm) strips.

Place a nori half on a bamboo mat lined up 1 inch (2.5 cm) away from the edge closest to you with the shiny side facing down and the indentations running vertically. Moisten your hands lightly with water and gently spread about ⅓ cup (75 ml) of the cauliflower rice evenly along the nori sheet, taking care not to compact it and leaving about a ½-inch (12-mm) border along the top and bottom of the nori sheet. Place one strip of salmon and a few strips of cucumber along the lower third of the nori.

Slip your thumbs under the edge of the bamboo mat closest to you. Use your thumbs to lift the mat and flip the edge of the nori and cauliflower rice over the filling, using your other fingers to press the filling toward you. Pull the mat forward, rolling to enclose the ingredients. Dip your finger in water and run it along the top of the exposed edge of the nori. Continue rolling to seal. Pull the mat over the roll and press to compress the roll.

Place the roll on a cutting board seam side down. Wet a sharp knife, trim the edges (cook's treat), then cut the roll into 4 or 6 pieces. Repeat with the remaining ingredients to make 6 rolls. Serve with small bowls of coconut aminos for dipping and spicy mayo, pickled ginger, and wasabi, if using.

SWAP

To make the rolls dairy-free and paleo: Omit the cream cheese.

smoky pork burrito bowl

SERVES 4

GLUTEN-FREE

GRAIN-FREE

PALEO

DAIRY-FREE

There are more than fifty thousand Mexican restaurants in the United States, but I don't know one that serves cauliflower rice in their burritos. This recipe is your grain-free solution.

It's equally delicious with Green Salsa (page 46), and you can swap chicken, beef, or another meat for the pork.

PORK

- 1 tablespoon extra-virgin olive oil
- 1 small green bell pepper, sliced
- 1 small red onion, sliced into half-moons
- 1 clove garlic, minced
- ½ teaspoon ground cumin
- ½ teaspoon ground chipotle chile
- 2 cups (390 g) shredded cooked pork
- 1½ cups (360 ml) Red Salsa (page 45), plus more for topping

CAULIFLOWER RICE

- 5 cups (650 g) Cauliflower Rice (page 36)
- 1 tablespoon extra-virgin olive oil
- ¼ teaspoon sea salt

GARNISHES

- 1 avocado, sliced
- 2 cups (110 g) shredded romaine lettuce
- ¼ cup (10 g) chopped fresh cilantro
- 1 lime, cut into 4 wedges (optional)
- Guacamole (page 156; optional), for serving

MAKE THE PORK: Heat the oil in a large skillet over medium-high heat. Add the bell pepper and onion and cook until crisp-tender, about 5 minutes. Add the garlic and cook for 1 minute, or until aromatic. Add the cumin and chipotle chile and cook for 30 seconds. Add the pork and cook to heat through. Add the salsa and stir to heat through.

MAKE THE CAULIFLOWER RICE: Heat the cauliflower rice in a large skillet over medium-high heat, stirring often, for 3 to 5 minutes to remove excess moisture. Add the oil and salt and cook for 1 minute more.

TO SERVE: Spoon the cauliflower rice into bowls. Put the pork on one side of the bowls and add the avocado and lettuce on the other side. Finish with more salsa and the cilantro and serve with a lime wedge and guacamole, if using, on the side.

cauliflower mash

SERVES 4 TO 6

GLUTEN-FREE

GRAIN-FREE

KETO FRIENDLY

VEGETARIAN

Making mashed potatoes out of cauliflower rice is a great way to feed cauliflower to a picky eater! When you add butter, milk, and sour cream, you'd be hard-pressed to notice the potatoes are missing from the mix. This recipe is reason enough to have cauliflower rice handy at all times. To make your mash even lower in carbs, sub in coconut milk for the dairy milk.

8 cups (1 kg) Cauliflower Rice (page 36)

2 tablespoons unsalted butter

¾ teaspoon sea salt, or to taste

2 cups (480 ml) milk

2 tablespoons sour cream

2 tablespoons Roasted Garlic Cream (optional; page 51)

1 tablespoon chopped fresh dill

Heat the cauliflower rice in a medium saucepan over medium-high heat, stirring often, for 3 to 5 minutes to remove excess moisture. Add the butter and salt and cook for 2 more minutes, stirring until the butter is completely melted. Add the milk, decrease the heat to medium, and cook for about 20 minutes, until all the liquid is absorbed. Stir in the sour cream. Add the garlic cream, if using. Remove from the heat. Using an immersion blender, blend on high speed for about 2 minutes, until the mash is smooth and creamy. Spoon into bowls, garnish with the dill, and serve.

skillets,

casseroles,

and

sheet pans

Our noodle-less lasagnas will change your conception of this classic casserole, the impossibly creamy quiche will cause you to swoon, and the shepherd's pie will bring you to a state of non-carb-induced bliss. This chapter is dedicated to one of my best friends, Cali'flour team member Stephanie Galland, who invented the Cali'flour lasagna.

meat lover's lasagna

SERVES 6

GLUTEN-FREE

GRAIN-FREE

KETO FRIENDLY

Our lasagnas are game changers. Not only are they easier to assemble than pasta lasagna (no boiling noodles!), but they are decidedly unfussy and no-fail because the cheese in the crust holds everything together.

- 1 (15-ounce/425-g) can tomato sauce
- ½ cup (120 ml) tomato paste
- 1 tablespoon dried oregano
- 1 tablespoon dried basil
- 1 teaspoon garlic powder
- 2 teaspoons extra-virgin olive oil
- 1 small yellow onion, chopped
- 5 cloves garlic, chopped
- 1 pound (455 g) ground beef
- ½ teaspoon sea salt
- ½ teaspoon freshly ground black pepper
- 1 teaspoon finely chopped fresh rosemary
- 1 teaspoon finely chopped fresh thyme
- 2 Cali'flour Pizza Crusts (page 26)
- 1 (15-ounce/425-g) container ricotta cheese
- 1 large egg
- ½ cup (10 g) fresh spinach leaves
- 4 ounces (115 g) low-moisture whole milk mozzarella cheese (not fresh), thinly sliced
- 5 fresh basil leaves
- ¼ cup (35 g) shredded Cheddar cheese
- ¼ cup (25 g) grated Parmesan cheese

Preheat the oven to 375°F (190°C).

In a medium saucepan, combine the tomato sauce, tomato paste, oregano, basil, and garlic powder. Bring to a simmer over medium heat, then reduce the heat to medium-low and simmer for 15 minutes, or until the beef in the next step is cooked.

While the sauce is cooking, heat the oil in a large skillet over medium heat. Add the onion and cook until softened, about 5 minutes. Add the fresh garlic and cook until softened, about 2 minutes. Add the beef and cook, stirring to break it up with a wooden spoon, until it is no longer pink and is starting to brown, about 10 minutes. Add the salt and pepper.

Transfer the beef to the pan of simmering sauce. Add the rosemary and thyme, stir well, and simmer for 10 minutes to combine the flavors.

Set one of the crusts in the bottom and slightly up the sides of a 9-inch (23-cm) round cake pan. Put the ricotta in a bowl and whisk the egg into it. Spread half of the ricotta mixture on top of the crust in the pan, then add half of the meat sauce and pack it down with a rubber spatula. Arrange the spinach on top. Place the second crust over the spinach, then add the remaining ricotta mixture, followed by the remaining meat sauce. Arrange the mozzarella cheese slices on top, followed by the basil leaves, then sprinkle with the Cheddar and Parmesan cheeses.

Place the pan on a baking sheet and bake for 30 minutes, or until the cheese is melted, bubbling, and lightly browned. Let rest for 10 to 15 minutes, then slice and serve.

pesto and roasted mushroom lasagna

SERVES 6

GLUTEN-FREE

GRAIN-FREE

KETO

VEGETARIAN

You don't even need to tell your guests that this lasagna is pasta-free—it's very unlikely they'll guess! Cali'flour lasagna is a great vehicle for getting even more veggies into your meals (remember, your "noodles" are made from cauliflower, so you're off to a great start), so once you've made my recipe, feel free to get creative and come up with your own signature veggie lasagnas. Note that the liquid from roasting the mushrooms is drained to keep the lasagna from getting soggy. Save the concentrated mushroom juices for flavoring soup such as French Onion Soup (page 102) or another vegetable dish.

1 pound (455 g) white mushrooms, sliced ¼ inch (6 mm) thick

1½ tablespoons extra-virgin olive oil

⅛ teaspoon sea salt

⅛ teaspoon freshly ground black pepper

1 sprig rosemary

2 Cali'flour Pizza Crusts (page 26)

1 (15-ounce/425-g) container ricotta cheese

1 large egg

1 cup (240 ml) Cauliflower Leaf Pesto (page 48)

1 cup (20 g) fresh spinach leaves

1 cup (110 g) shredded low-moisture whole milk mozzarella cheese (not fresh)

¼ cup (25 g) grated Parmesan cheese

Pinch of paprika

Preheat the oven to 375°F (190°C).

Put the mushrooms in a large bowl and toss with the oil. Add the salt and pepper and toss again. Spread the mushrooms over a baking sheet and place the rosemary sprig on top. Roast for about 10 minutes, until the mushrooms release a good amount of liquid. Carefully drain the liquid, then return to the oven and roast for about 20 minutes more, stirring once or twice, until the mushrooms are browned, fairly dry, and softened but still hold their shape. Remove and discard the rosemary.

Set one of the crusts onto in the bottom and slightly up the sides of a 9-inch (23-cm) round cake pan. Put the ricotta in a bowl and whisk the egg into it with a fork to combine. Spread ½ cup (120 ml) of the pesto on top of the crust, then dollop half of the ricotta mixture over the pesto and use a rubber spatula to spread it evenly. Top with the mushrooms, followed by the spinach. Place the second crust over the spinach, then spread the remaining ½ cup (120 ml) pesto on top. Dollop the remaining ricotta mixture over the pesto and spread it out (it's OK if some of the pesto shows). Scatter the mozzarella on top, then add the Parmesan. Sprinkle with the paprika.

Place the pan on a baking sheet and bake for 30 minutes, or until the cheese is melted, bubbling, and slightly browned. Let rest for 10 to 15 minutes, then slice and serve.

quiche lorraine

SERVES 6

GLUTEN-FREE

GRAIN-FREE

KETO FRIENDLY

The most challenging part of making quiche is the crust. Here two Cali'flour pizza crusts join forces to provide a built-in crust. This may be the creamiest quiche you've ever eaten—the crème fraîche makes all the difference.

- 2 Cali'flour Pizza Crusts (page 26)
- 8 strips bacon
- 3 large eggs
- 1 large egg yolk
- 1 cup (240 ml) heavy cream
- ½ cup (120 ml) crème fraîche
- ¼ teaspoon sea salt
- ¼ teaspoon freshly ground black pepper, plus more for topping
- 3 ounces (85 g) Gruyère cheese, shredded
- Thyme leaves for garnish

Preheat the oven to 375°F (190°C).

Set one of the crusts in a 10-inch (25-cm) pie pan. Cut the second crust into 4 strips and lay them inside the rim of the pan touching the bottom crust. Press the strips into the bottom crust to loosely connect them.

Lay the bacon on a baking sheet. Put the crust on the top rack of the oven and the bacon on the bottom rack and bake until the crust is browned and the bacon is crisp, about 15 minutes.

Remove the bacon from the pan to a paper towel–lined plate to drain (save the fat for another recipe). Place the pie pan on a wire rack to cool until just warm.

In a large bowl, beat the eggs, egg yolk, cream, and crème fraîche to combine. Beat in the salt and pepper.

Crumble the bacon and spread it over the crust. Sprinkle the cheese on top. Pour the egg mixture into the pan and place on a baking sheet. Make aluminum foil tents for any exposed crust. Place in the oven and bake until lightly golden and a knife blade inserted about 1 inch (2.5 cm) from the edge comes out almost fully clean and the center feels set but soft like gelatin, 30 to 40 minutes. Sprinkle with pepper and thyme leaves and transfer the quiche to a wire rack to cool for at least 20 minutes. Serve warm or at room temperature.

SWAP

To make this quiche vegetarian: Omit the bacon.

lamb and sweet potato shepherd's pie

SERVES 6

GLUTEN-FREE

GRAIN-FREE

KETO FRIENDLY

Fun fact: New Zealand, where my husband Jim's family is from, has the highest density of sheep in the world. The country is the largest exporter of lamb. When we go to New Zealand to visit we find lamb pies everywhere, from dressy restaurants to the mini case at the gas station. Here this classic meat-and-potato dish goes spudless and leaves you feeling surprisingly light after your meal.

1½ pounds (680 g) ground lamb

1 onion, chopped

4 ounces (115 g) white mushrooms, including stems, chopped

2 cloves garlic, finely chopped

1 tablespoon tomato paste

2 tablespoons red wine

1 cup (240 ml) beef or chicken stock

2 teaspoons Worcestershire sauce

2 teaspoons fresh thyme leaves

2 teaspoons chopped fresh rosemary

1 small sweet potato, grated

½ teaspoon sea salt

¼ teaspoon freshly ground black pepper, plus more for dusting

1 tablespoon arrowroot powder

1 recipe Cauliflower Mash (page 132)

2 large egg yolks

2 teaspoons chopped fresh dill

Adjust the oven rack about 5 inches (12 cm) from the broiler element and preheat the broiler.

In a 10-inch (25-cm) oven-proof skillet, combine the lamb, onion, mushrooms, and garlic. Place over medium-high heat and cook, stirring often to break up the lamb, until the fat releases from the lamb and the juices release from the mushrooms and then dry out, about 20 minutes. Carefully tip the pan over a bowl and remove as much of the fat as you can.

Stir the tomato paste into the lamb and cook, stirring often, for 2 minutes. Add the wine and cook, stirring to break up any browned bits, until evaporated, about 1 minute. Add the stock, Worcestershire sauce, thyme, rosemary, sweet potato, salt, and pepper. Bring to a simmer, then reduce the heat to medium and cook until the stock is almost fully absorbed and the sweet potato is softened, about 10 minutes. Put the arrowroot in a small bowl and stir in 1 tablespoon cold water to dissolve it. Add the arrowroot to the pan, cook for 1 minute, then remove from the heat.

Put the cauliflower mash in a large bowl and whisk in the egg yolks. Transfer to a zip-top bag and snip off one corner to create a 1-inch (2.5-cm) opening. Pipe the mash over the filling, covering it completely, going back in and filling in gaps as needed. Smooth the mash with the back of a spoon (use the spoon to create soft peaks if you like). Dust with pepper. Place the skillet on a baking sheet and broil until the mash is browned in places and the filling is bubbly, about 10 minutes. Remove from the oven and top with the dill. Let cool for 10 minutes before serving.

chicken and black bean enchilada casserole

SERVES 6

GLUTEN-FREE

GRAIN-FREE

This recipe is inspired by a dish Nicole Mimbs, of the Cali'flour team, made for our YouTube channel. Once you have the ingredients prepped, it takes just five minutes to assemble this casserole. Nicole is a busy mom, so cooking quick, healthy meals like this one is very important to her. Nicole embodies unconditional friendship and love (and she has even taught me to love Brussels sprouts!), and I am grateful for her role in the success of Cali'flour Foods.

Note: You'll need two batches of salsa for this saucy casserole, or you could sub in a store-bought salsa for convenience.

- 2 cups (185 g) shredded cooked chicken
- 1 (15-ounce/425-g) can black beans, drained and rinsed
- 1 (4-ounce/115-g) can chopped green chiles, drained
- 2 cups (230 g) shredded Monterey Jack cheese
- 3 cups (720 ml) Green Salsa (page 46)
- 2 Cali'flour Pizza Crusts (page 26)
- 1 small avocado, sliced
- 1 scallion (white and green parts), thinly sliced

Preheat the oven to 375°F (190°C).

In a large bowl, combine the chicken, beans, chiles, 1 cup (115 g) of the cheese, and 1 cup (240 ml) of the salsa. Spread ½ cup (120 ml) of the remaining salsa over the bottom of a 9-inch (23-cm) round cake pan. Set one of the crusts into the bottom and slightly up the sides of the pan. Cover with the chicken mixture, then set the second crust on top. Top with the remaining 1½ cups (360 ml) salsa and 1 cup (115 g) cheese and sprinkle with the scallion. Place the pan on a baking sheet and bake for 30 minutes, or until the cheese is melted, bubbling, and lightly browned. Let rest for 10 to 15 minutes, top with the avocado and scallion, then slice and serve.

cauliflower steak with roasted cauliflower leaves

SERVES 4

GLUTEN-FREE
GRAIN-FREE
PALEO
KETO FRIENDLY
VEGAN
VEGETARIAN
DAIRY-FREE

When you have a hankering for cauliflower pure and simple, make it cauliflower steak night! You can make your steak in a cast-iron pan or even cook it out on the barbecue. A side of roasted cauliflower leaves completes the "steak and salad" pairing. I like to slice my cauliflower steak horizontally rather than top to bottom to yield several smaller steaks revealing beautiful flower shapes on all sides. Note that the amount of cauliflower leaves and their size and texture will vary from head to head. Chop larger leaves to make them easier to bite into. Serve your steak on its own or with Plant-Based Pesto (page 50), White Sauce (page 44), Marinara Sauce (page 40), or the condiment of your choosing.

1 large head cauliflower, core trimmed, leaves chopped if large

3 tablespoons extra-virgin olive oil

Sea salt and freshly ground black pepper

Sprinkle of spices or herbs such as turmeric, cumin, or celery seed

Preheat the oven to 400°F (205°C).

Place the cauliflower leaves on a baking sheet and toss with 1 tablespoon of the oil. Season with salt and pepper. Roast for about 15 minutes, until the greens darken and turn crispy. Remove from the oven and increase the oven temperature to 450°F (230°C). Leave the leaves on the pan while you make the steaks.

Place a second baking sheet in the oven to heat for 10 minutes. Add 1 tablespoon of the remaining oil to the pan. Slice the cauliflower horizontally about ¾ inch (2 cm) thick and add the slices to the pan. Brush with the remaining 1 tablespoon oil and sprinkle with salt and pepper and your choice of seasonings. Roast for 10 minutes, or until browned on the bottom, then flip and roast for another 10 minutes, or until browned all over. Return the cauliflower leaves to the oven for about 2 minutes to heat through. Serve the steaks with the leaves and your choice of topping.

small bites and party food

I love to throw parties, and I've done them in every theme, from murder mysteries to Mardi Gras, so small bites are a big part of my life. I didn't want my lupus diagnosis to keep me from eating the same foods as my guests, so I got creative and now invite a certain secret guest to my parties! Whether it's popcorn, hummus, or nachos, I know cauliflower's got me covered.

cauliflower popcorn

SERVES 2

GLUTEN-FREE
GRAIN-FREE
PALEO
KETO
VEGAN
VEGETARIAN
DAIRY-FREE

Salty, crunchy bits of cauliflower need no disguise for your family to make a habit out of them! For maximum crispness, eat them right after they come out of the oven. The recipe scales up easily, so you can have plenty ready for movie night.

1 small head cauliflower

3 tablespoons extra-virgin olive oil

2 tablespoons nutritional yeast

½ teaspoon garlic powder

¼ teaspoon sea salt

Preheat the oven to 475°F (245°C).

Cut the cauliflower into quarters through the core, then cut out the core and leaves from each quarter in one cut. Trim any remaining core and leaves. Break the florets into 2-inch (5-cm) or so pieces and cut the stems as close to the florets as possible. Using your hands, break off popcorn-size pieces of cauliflower, trimming away any remaining stem.

Put the florets in a zip-top bag and toss with the oil. In a small bowl, combine the nutritional yeast, garlic powder, and salt. Add to the cauliflower and toss to coat.

Spread the cauliflower out on a baking sheet in a single layer and roast, stirring halfway through, until softened and well browned, 15 to 20 minutes. Serve immediately.

VARIATION

Smoky Cauliflower Popcorn: *Add ¼ teaspoon ground chipotle chile.*

new classic hummus

MAKES ABOUT 3 CUPS (720 ML)

GLUTEN-FREE

GRAIN-FREE

PALEO

KETO FRIENDLY

VEGAN

VEGETARIAN

DAIRY-FREE

This recipe takes hummus to new heights by swapping roasted cauliflower for chickpeas but keeping the traditional tahini, lemon, herbs, and spices that give it its iconic flavor. For an impromptu pizza, simply spread some over a crust and top with salad veggies, a drizzle of olive oil, a squeeze of lemon, and a pinch of salt. A high-speed blender will give you the smoothest results. This recipe is inspired by the many bowls of hummus Stephanie Galland, queen of small bites and party food, has shared with me.

1 cup (130 g) raw cashews

3 cups (300 g) 2-inch (5-cm) cauliflower florets

4 tablespoons extra-virgin olive oil, plus more for drizzling

1¼ teaspoons sea salt, or to taste

¾ cup (180 ml) tahini (sesame paste)

2 teaspoons grated lemon zest

¼ cup (60 ml) fresh lemon juice, or to taste

3 cloves garlic, chopped

1 teaspoon ground cumin

¼ teaspoon freshly ground black pepper, or to taste

⅛ teaspoon cayenne pepper

⅓ cup (15 g) chopped fresh cilantro, plus more for garnish

Paprika for garnish

Put the cashews in a medium bowl and add hot water to cover by a couple of inches. Cover with a dish towel and leave to soak for at least 1 hour or up to overnight. Drain.

Preheat the oven to 450°F (230°C).

Put the cauliflower in a large bowl and add 1 tablespoon of the oil and ¼ teaspoon of the salt. Toss to coat and spread over a baking sheet. Roast, stirring once or twice, until the cauliflower is browned in places and tender. Transfer to a food processor or blender; add the remaining 3 tablespoons oil, the tahini, 6 tablespoons (90 ml) water, the lemon zest, lemon juice, garlic, cumin, the remaining 1 teaspoon salt, the black pepper, and cayenne; and process until smooth, scraping the sides as needed and adding more water if it is too thick, 3 to 5 minutes. Spoon into a bowl, drizzle with oil, garnish with cilantro and paprika, and serve. The hummus will keep, covered and refrigerated, for up to 5 days.

VARIATIONS

Beet and Balsamic Hummus: *Blend in 1 large roasted beet (chopped) and a splash of good balsamic vinegar, to taste.*

Za'atar Hummus: *Swap the cilantro for parsley and add 2 teaspoons za'atar. Finish with a sprinkle of za'atar.*

smoky eggplant dip

MAKES ABOUT 1½ CUPS (360 ML)

Burning the heck out of whole eggplant causes the flesh to collapse into creamy submission, with the flesh taking on incredibly smoky notes while remaining uncharred. The dip is improved only by a sprinkle of cauliflower-based breadcrumbs and chips. To keep the dish both vegan and paleo, use the Plant-Based crust (page 28) for your breadcrumbs and chips. You could repurpose the dip to make a sandwich, panini, wrap, or quesadilla, or make a pizza out of it (see the variation at right). The recipe easily doubles for your entertaining needs.

- 2 large eggplants
- 2 tablespoons extra-virgin olive oil
- 1 tablespoon fresh lemon juice, or to taste
- 1 large clove garlic, pressed through a garlic press
- ½ teaspoon sea salt, or to taste
- ½ teaspoon freshly ground black pepper
- 1 scallion (white and green parts), thinly sliced
- 2 tablespoons minced red bell pepper
- 3 tablespoons Cali'flour Breadcrumbs (page 35; optional)
- Cali'flour Chips (page 34), for serving

Preheat the broiler and line a broiler pan with aluminum foil.

Spear the eggplants with a paring knife several times about ½ inch (12 mm) deep. Place on the prepared pan and broil for 30 to 45 minutes (broilers can vary widely), turning them once, until the skin is burnt to a crisp and the flesh is collapsed.

Remove from the broiler to a plate, break open the skin to release steam, and cool slightly. Remove the flesh from the skin and discard the skin. Chop the flesh and drain it in a mesh strainer set over a bowl for about 1 hour to release excess liquid.

Put the eggplant in a medium bowl and add the oil, lemon juice, garlic, salt, and black pepper. Set aside for 30 minutes to marinate. Spoon into a serving bowl, top with the scallion, bell pepper, and breadcrumbs, if using, and serve with chips for dipping.

GLUTEN-FREE
GRAIN-FREE
PALEO
KETO FRIENDLY
VEGAN
VEGETARIAN
DAIRY-FREE

VARIATION

Deconstructed Ratatouille Pizza: *Spread ½ cup (120 ml) eggplant dip over a cooked pizza crust and top with 1 small tomato, sliced. Add 1 roasted red bell pepper, cut into thin strips. Bake in a preheated 425°F (220°C) oven for 8 to 10 minutes, until hot, and garnish with 1 tablespoon torn fresh basil leaves.*

new classic hummus

smoky eggplant dip

beef nachos

SERVES 4

GLUTEN-FREE

GRAIN-FREE

KETO

My oldest son, James, won't touch vegetables, but he's a nacho-holic, and beef nachos are his favorite. With a Cali'flour pizza crust as a nacho base, I no longer need to nag him to eat his veggies! Make the salsa a little wetter (by adding juices from the tomato can) than if you were spreading it over pizza. For added kick, make the chips with a Spicy Jalapeño crust (page 26). You can also make your nachos with ground turkey or pork.

GUACAMOLE

- 2 avocados
- ½ small tomato, chopped (optional)
- ¼ small red onion, minced
- ¼ teaspoon sea salt, or to taste
- 2 tablespoons chopped fresh cilantro
- 2 teaspoons fresh lime juice, or to taste

NACHOS

- ½ recipe Cali'flour Chips (page 34)
- ½ cup (55 g) shredded Cheddar cheese
- ½ cup (60 g) cooked ground beef
- ½ cup (120 ml) Red Salsa (page 45)
- 1 small jalapeño chile, sliced (optional)
- 2 scallions (white and green parts), chopped
- 1 tablespoon chopped fresh cilantro
- 2 tablespoons sour cream

MAKE THE GUACAMOLE: Cut the avocados in half and remove the pits. Scoop out the avocado flesh and put it in a medium bowl. Using the back of a fork, mash the avocado until as chunky or smooth as you like it. Mix in the tomato (if using), onion, salt, and cilantro. Stir in the lime juice. Taste and season with more salt and/or lime juice if needed.

MAKE THE NACHOS: Preheat the oven to 375°F (190°C).

Place half of the chips in the bottom of a medium cast-iron skillet. Sprinkle with 3 tablespoons of the cheese, followed by ¼ cup (30 g) of the beef, then ¼ cup (60 ml) of the salsa and half of the chile, if using. Repeat the layering, then finish with the remaining 2 tablespoons cheese.

Place in the oven and bake for about 10 minutes, until the cheese is melted. Top with the scallions and cilantro. Dollop the sour cream on top and add the guacamole to the sides for dipping. Serve immediately, straight from the skillet.

buffalo cauliflower

SERVES 4

GLUTEN-FREE

GRAIN-FREE

KETO FRIENDLY

VEGETARIAN

My hometown of Chico, California, is a huge football town, and we boast Aaron Rodgers as a native. The quarterback attended Pleasant Valley High School, where my kids go. The Super Bowl is a fun time for us to sit back and enjoy this healthy spin on a favorite that skips the deep fryer for some serious cauliflower love.

CAULIFLOWER

- ¾ cup (85 g) almond flour
- 2 teaspoons garlic powder
- 1 teaspoon onion powder
- ½ teaspoon sea salt
- 2 large eggs
- 1 (2-pound/910-g) head cauliflower
- Extra-virgin olive oil cooking spray

BUFFALO SAUCE

- ½ cup (120 ml) hot pepper sauce, such as Frank's
- 2 tablespoons salted or unsalted butter

BLUE CHEESE DIP

- ½ cup (70 g) crumbled blue cheese
- ¼ cup (60 ml) sour cream
- 2 tablespoons buttermilk
- 2 tablespoons mayonnaise
- 2 teaspoons white wine vinegar
- Pinch of sea salt

FOR SERVING

- Celery sticks

MAKE THE CAULIFLOWER: Preheat the oven to 450°F (230°C) and line a baking sheet with parchment paper.

In a large zip-top bag, combine the almond flour, garlic powder, onion powder, and ¼ teaspoon of the salt. In a large bowl, beat the eggs with the remaining ¼ teaspoon salt.

Cut the cauliflower into quarters through the core, then cut out the core and leaves from each quarter in one cut. Trim any remaining core and leaves. Break the cauliflower into approximately 2-inch (5-cm) florets. Add the cauliflower to the egg mixture and mix to thoroughly coat. Transfer to the bag with the flour and shake until the cauliflower is well coated.

Transfer the cauliflower to the prepared baking sheet with a little space between the pieces and spray with cooking spray. Bake for 20 minutes, or until the cauliflower is starting to brown, then flip the pieces and bake for another 10 minutes, or until well browned all over.

While the cauliflower is in the oven, MAKE THE BUFFALO SAUCE: In a small saucepan, combine the hot pepper sauce and butter and cook, stirring, over low heat until the butter is melted.

MAKE THE BLUE CHEESE DIP: Combine all the ingredients in a small bowl and mix with a fork until the cheese is well incorporated.

TO SERVE: Place the roasted cauliflower in a serving bowl, pour the buffalo sauce on top, and toss to coat. Serve immediately, with the dip and celery sticks.

veggie pizzas

I used to equate pizza with pepperoni, but in the early days of the business, we witnessed a huge growth in demand for veggie pizzas. At the Chico Farmers' Market, we'd put out samples of pepperoni, cheese, and veggie-loaded Cali'flour pizzas, and the ones with the most veggies were always the first to go. People were looking for dishes to match their plant-forward lifestyles and make use of seasonal farmers' market produce. The pizzas we came up with back then, from my famous stir-fry to the zoodle alfredo, were the inspiration for the recipes in this chapter.

margherita pizza

SERVES 3

GLUTEN-FREE

GRAIN-FREE

KETO FRIENDLY

VEGETARIAN

The classic revisited to satisfy your deepest cravings with fewer carbs. Thank you, oh mighty cauliflower! Consider freezing ¼-cup (60-ml) bags of Marinara Sauce so you're always just one step from your next Margherita.

- 1 Cali'flour Pizza Crust (page 26)
- ¼ cup (60 ml) Marinara Sauce (page 40)
- 2 ounces (55 g) mozzarella cheese, thinly sliced
- ½ small to medium tomato, thinly sliced
- Fresh basil leaves

Preheat the oven to 425°F (220°C). Line a baking sheet with parchment paper or get out your pizza pan and put your crust on it.

Spread the sauce over the crust and top with the cheese. Place the tomato slices over the cheese. Bake for 8 to 10 minutes, until the cheese is melted. Remove to a serving plate, top with the basil, then slice and serve.

VARIATIONS

Ricotta Margherita: *Dollop 2 tablespoons ricotta cheese onto the pizza.*

Garlicky Margherita: *Spread 2 tablespoons Roasted Garlic Cream (page 51) over the crust before adding the marinara sauce.*

garlicky double cauliflower pizza

SERVES 3, WITH EXTRA GARLICKY CAULIFLOWER

GLUTEN-FREE

GRAIN-FREE

KETO

VEGETARIAN

One of cauliflower's superpowers is to take on the flavors it's cooked with—for this pizza topping, ample garlic and oregano. This is a pizza for cauliflower lovers who don't need to hide it to appreciate it! You'll have cauliflower topping left over for additional pizzas or to toss with grain-free pasta, a glug of olive oil, and a squeeze of lemon for a quick meal. In season, consider scattering quartered cherry tomatoes on top for a juicy, tangy pop of red.

GARLICKY CAULIFLOWER (MAKES ABOUT 4 CUPS/700 G)

2 tablespoons extra-virgin olive oil

3 cloves garlic, sliced

1 medium head (about 2½ pounds/1.2 kg) cauliflower, cut into florets, stems chopped

½ teaspoon sea salt

1 teaspoon dried oregano

3 tablespoons grated Parmesan cheese

PIZZA

1 Cali'flour Pizza Crust (page 26)

¼ cup (60 ml) Cauliflower Leaf Pesto (page 48)

1 tablespoon toasted pine nuts

1 teaspoon grated Parmesan cheese

Red pepper flakes (optional)

Handful of pea shoots, baby arugula, or microgreens

1 teaspoon extra-virgin olive oil

Squeeze of fresh lemon juice

MAKE THE GARLICKY CAULIFLOWER: Combine the oil and garlic in a large sauté pan and cook over low heat, stirring occasionally, for about 5 minutes, until the garlic is light golden in color.

Increase the heat to medium-low and add the cauliflower and salt. Cover and cook, stirring occasionally, for 20 minutes, or until the cauliflower is soft but not falling apart and just slightly colored. Add a little water if it starts to stick to the bottom of the pan. Uncover, add the oregano, and cook, stirring often, for 5 minutes. Stir in the cheese. Using a potato masher or the back of a wooden spoon, mash or break up the cauliflower into a chunky mash. Let cool slightly.

MAKE THE PIZZA: Preheat the oven to 425°F (220°C). Line a baking sheet with parchment paper or get out your pizza pan and put your crust on it.

Spread the pesto (loosen it with a little water or oil if it's too thick for spreading) over the crust and top with ½ cup (87 g) garlicky cauliflower. Place in the oven and bake for 8 to 10 minutes, until everything is hot. Remove from the oven to a cutting board and sprinkle with the pine nuts, cheese, and red pepper flakes, if using. Arrange the pea shoots on top and finish with the oil and lemon juice. Slice and serve.

SWAPS

To make this pizza vegan: Use a Plant-Based crust (page 28), Plant-Based Parmesan Cheese (page 55) as your cheese, and sub in Plant-Based Pesto (page 50) for the Cauliflower Leaf Pesto.

pan-roasted lemon broccoli pizza

SERVES 3

GLUTEN-FREE

GRAIN-FREE

PALEO

KETO

VEGAN

VEGETARIAN

DAIRY-FREE

Like my oldest son, James, I didn't like many vegetables growing up. Rice cereal and fish sticks were my reason for eating, but broccoli was an exception. I was a fan then, and I continue to be, and who wouldn't love broccoli when you toss it with pesto and serve it on a pizza!

- 1 Plant-Based Cali'flour Pizza Crust (page 28)
- 1 tablespoon extra-virgin olive oil
- 1½ cups (about 5 ounces/140 g) small broccoli florets (about the size of a quarter)
- Sea salt and freshly ground black pepper
- ½ small lemon
- ¼ cup (60 ml) Plant-Based Pesto (page 50)
- 2 teaspoons Plant-Based Parmesan Cheese (page 55; optional)
- Pinch of red pepper flakes (optional)

Preheat the oven to 425°F (220°C). Line a baking sheet with parchment paper or get out your pizza pan and put your crust on it.

Heat the oil in a medium skillet with a lid over medium-high heat. Add the broccoli in an even layer and sprinkle with ⅛ teaspoon salt and a pinch of pepper. Lay the lemon half cut side down on the pan. Cover and cook without stirring for 2 minutes, or until the broccoli is well browned on the bottom and crisp-tender throughout. Remove from the heat.

Spread the pesto over the crust and arrange the broccoli on top. Place in the oven and bake for 8 to 10 minutes, until everything is hot. Remove from the oven to a cutting board, sprinkle with the cheese and red pepper flakes, if using, and squeeze the lemon half over the top. Finish with a pinch of salt and pepper, then slice and serve.

VARIATION

Broccoli, Marinara, and Ricotta Pizza: *Use Marinara Sauce (page 40) in place of the pesto and dollop 1 tablespoon Almond Ricotta (page 58) on top after the pizza comes out of the oven.*

detox pizza

SERVES 3

GLUTEN-FREE
GRAIN-FREE
PALEO
KETO
VEGAN
VEGETARIAN
DAIRY-FREE

Shiitake mushrooms, cilantro, and broccoli sprouts are all superfood immune boosters. Shiitake mushrooms fight against inflammation, tumors, heart disease, and viruses. Cilantro can bind to heavy metals in the bloodstream to purify the whole body. And broccoli sprouts can help us detox from environmental pollution. Add the three to a pizza containing cauliflower, and pizza night doubles as detox night! As a bonus, bitter dandelion greens give your liver a spring cleaning, and the pizza contains a whole head of garlic—just the thing to ward off colds and strengthen your entire system.

- 1 Plant-Based Cali'flour Pizza Crust (page 28)
- 4 shiitake mushroom caps, very thinly sliced
- 3 teaspoons extra-virgin olive oil
- 2 pinches of flaky sea salt
- 2 tablespoons Roasted Garlic Cream (page 51)
- ¼ cup (5 g) dandelion greens
- ¼ cup (12 g) broccoli sprouts or other sprouts
- 2 tablespoons spiralized, shaved, or julienned carrots
- 6 fresh cilantro leaves, torn
- ½ teaspoon grated lemon zest
- Squeeze of fresh lemon juice
- Freshly ground black pepper

Preheat the oven to 425°F (220°C). Line a baking sheet with parchment paper or get out your pizza pan and put your crust on it.

Put the mushrooms in a small bowl, add 1 teaspoon of the oil and a pinch of salt, and lightly massage them with your hands to start to soften them.

Spread the garlic cream over the crust and top with the mushrooms. Place in the oven and bake for 8 to 10 minutes, until the pizza is hot and the mushrooms are softened. Remove from the oven to a cutting board and arrange the dandelion greens, sprouts, carrots, and cilantro over the top. Finish with the lemon zest and juice, a few grinds of the peppermill, and the remaining pinch of salt. Drizzle with the remaining 2 teaspoons oil, then slice and serve.

white bean and smashed rosemary roasted cherry tomato pizza

SERVES 3, WITH EXTRA ROASTED CHERRY TOMATOES

GLUTEN-FREE

GRAIN-FREE

KETO

VEGAN

VEGETARIAN

DAIRY-FREE

Roasting cherry tomatoes concentrates their tomato flavor, and then they burst and release their sweet, tart juices to make a deliciously chunky topping for pizza. A layer of white bean spread serves as a creamy protein source, and two plant-based cheeses are the finishing touch.

ROASTED CHERRY TOMATOES (MAKES ABOUT ¾ CUP/350 G)

- 1 pint cherry tomatoes
- 1 tablespoon extra-virgin olive oil
- ¼ teaspoon red wine vinegar
- ½ teaspoon chopped fresh rosemary
- ⅛ teaspoon sea salt
- Pinch of freshly ground black pepper

PIZZA

- 1 Plant-Based Cali'flour Pizza Crust (page 28)
- ⅓ cup (75 ml) White Bean Spread (page 54)
- 2 tablespoons Almond Ricotta (page 58)
- 1 teaspoon Plant-Based Parmesan Cheese (page 55)
- ½ teaspoon fresh thyme leaves, or 3 torn fresh parsley leaves

MAKE THE ROASTED CHERRY TOMATOES: Preheat the oven to 425°F (220°C).

In a medium ovenproof skillet, toss the tomatoes with the oil. Place in the oven and roast for about 20 minutes, turning a couple times and lightly smashing them with a wooden spoon to collapse them and thicken their juices, about 20 minutes. Transfer to a bowl and add the vinegar, rosemary, salt, and pepper.

MAKE THE PIZZA: Increase the oven temperature to 425°F (220°C). Line a baking sheet with parchment paper or get out your pizza pan and put your crust on it.

Spread the white bean spread over the crust and top with ¼ cup (117 g) roasted cherry tomatoes. Place in the oven and bake for 8 to 10 minutes, until everything is hot. Remove from the oven to a serving plate, top with small dollops of the ricotta, sprinkle on the Parmesan, and scatter the thyme on top. Slice and serve.

SWAPS

To make this pizza paleo: Omit the white bean spread and double the roasted cherry tomatoes.

To make this pizza vegetarian (rather than vegan): Use dairy ricotta and Parmesan cheese.

tahini beet pizza

SERVES 3

GLUTEN-FREE
GRAIN-FREE
PALEO
KETO FRIENDLY
VEGAN
VEGETARIAN
DAIRY-FREE

Smashing beets creates a textured surface to welcome in a limey, garlicky tahini sauce. You could also sub in sweet potatoes or carrots for the beets, and if your beets came with their greens, julienne a handful to use as a garnish. It's easiest to smash the beets while they are still warm from the oven.

1 Plant-Based Cali'flour Pizza Crust (page 28)

2 small red beets, roasted or steamed (see below)

4 tablespoons (60 ml) Creamy Tahini Sauce (page 152)

2 teaspoons chopped fresh flat-leaf parsley

Pinch of flaky sea salt

Squeeze of fresh lime juice

Preheat the oven to 425°F (220°C). Line a baking sheet with parchment paper or get out your pizza pan and put your crust on it.

Place the beets on a cutting board or plate and press on them with a potato masher or the bottom of a sturdy measuring cup until they are smashed (but not mashed) with an uneven surface area.

Spread 3 tablespoons of the tahini sauce over the crust and cover with the beets. Place in the oven and bake for 8 to 10 minutes, until everything is hot. Remove from the oven to a cutting board, drizzle with the remaining 1 tablespoon tahini, and finish with the parsley, salt, and lime juice. Slice and serve.

How to Roast or Steam Beets

Remove the greens from the beets and scrub the beets clean.

To roast beets: Wrap the beets individually in aluminum foil, place in a roasting pan, and roast in a preheated 375°F (190°C) oven for about 1 hour, until the beets can be easily pierced with a thin knife. Cool slightly and use your fingers or a paper towel to remove the skins.

To steam beets: Place the beets in a steamer basket set in a saucepan to fit with about 1 inch (2.5 cm) of water. Cover and bring to a boil over high heat, then lower the heat to medium and steam for 35 to 40 minutes, until the beets can be easily pierced with a thin knife. Cool slightly and use your fingers or a paper towel to remove the skins.

VARIATION

Golden Beet and Pink Peppercorn Pizza: *Sub golden beets for the red and finish with a splash of balsamic vinegar and ½ teaspoon crushed pink peppercorns.*

avocado and red salsa pizza

SERVES 3

GLUTEN-FREE
GRAIN-FREE
PALEO
KETO
VEGAN
VEGETARIAN
DAIRY-FREE

My take on guac and salsa is loaded with fresh, clean flavors plus extra jalapeños for kick. To take it up another notch, use a Spicy Jalapeño crust (page 26).

- ½ cup (120 ml) Red Salsa (page 45)
- 1 Plant-Based Cali'flour Crust (page 28), baked a little longer than specified in the recipe
- ½ avocado, sliced
- ½ small jalapeño chile, cut in half and sliced
- Squeeze of fresh lime juice
- Handful fresh cilantro leaves
- Pinch of flaky sea salt

Spread the salsa over the crust. Arrange the avocado over the crust and sprinkle with the jalapeño. Drizzle the lime juice the top and finish with the cilantro and salt. Slice and serve.

SWAP

To make this pizza vegetarian (rather than vegan): Use a Cali'flour crust (page 26) and top with 2 tablespoons crumbled cotija or feta cheese.

VARIATION

Avocado and Green Salsa Pizza: *Swap Green Salsa (page 46) for the red.*

mexican street food salad pizza

SERVES 3

GLUTEN-FREE

GRAIN-FREE

KETO

VEGETARIAN

This street food turned pizza is simple yet bold, with multiple taste and texture bases covered, from smoky to limey, creamy, and cheesy. It replaces the traditional corn with zucchini to make it paleo friendly. To up the heat, use a Spicy Jalapeño crust (page 26).

1 Cali'flour Pizza Crust (page 26)

⅓ cup (40 g) cubed zucchini (¼-inch/6-mm cubes)

2 tablespoons mayonnaise

1 clove garlic, pressed through a garlic press

Large pinch of sea salt

3 tablespoons finely crumbled feta or cotija cheese

1 tablespoon very thinly slivered red onion

⅛ teaspoon cayenne pepper (optional)

⅛ teaspoon ground cumin

1 teaspoon minced red chile

Handful fresh cilantro leaves

Squeeze of fresh lime juice

Preheat the oven to 425°F (220°C). Line a baking sheet with parchment paper or get out your pizza pan and put your crust on it.

Heat a large skillet, preferably cast iron, over medium-high heat. Add the zucchini and cook until browned in places, 4 to 5 minutes. Remove from the pan to a plate and cool.

In a small bowl, whisk together the mayonnaise, garlic, and salt. Spread the mixture over the crust. Scatter 2 tablespoons of the cheese, the zucchini, and onion over the crust and bake for about 8 minutes, until the cheese is mostly melted. Remove from the oven to a serving plate and sprinkle with the remaining 1 tablespoon cheese, the cayenne, if using, and cumin. Scatter the red chile and cilantro on top and finish with the lime juice. Slice and serve.

SWAP

To make this pizza vegan: Use a Plant-Based crust (page 28) and vegan mayonnaise and swap Plant-Based Parmesan Cheese (page 55) for the feta.

zoodle alfredo pizza

SERVES 3

GLUTEN-FREE
GRAIN-FREE
PALEO
KETO FRIENDLY
VEGAN
VEGETARIAN
DAIRY-FREE

When I started selling my pizza crusts at the Chico Farmers' Market, I also offered zucchini noodles—aka zoodles—before they were ever in grocery stores. When it came time to take my business to the next step, I had to choose between zoodles and cauliflower pizza because I didn't have the money, equipment, or manpower for both. Shortly after I launched Cali'flour Foods, zoodles went through the roof, but our pizzas aren't doing too shabby either! I still love taking out the spiralizer and making zoodles, and here I've combined my first two veggie loves in this dairy-free pizza made with a cauliflower take on alfredo sauce.

1 small zucchini, spiralized into spaghetti or wide noodle shapes (or 2 cups/150 g packaged zucchini noodles)

½ cup (120 ml) White Sauce (page 44)

1 Plant-Based Cali'flour Pizza Crust (page 28), baked for a few minutes longer than specified in the recipe

2 teaspoons Plant-Based Parmesan Cheese (page 55)

½ teaspoon dried garlic flakes (optional)

Red pepper flakes (optional)

Heat a small skillet over medium-high heat. Add the zucchini noodles and cook until slightly softened, about 2 minutes. Add the white sauce and toss to coat and warm the sauce through. Spread the noodles and sauce over the crust. Top with the cheese and garlic flakes and red pepper flakes, if using. Slice and serve.

spinach and artichoke dip pizza

SERVES 3

GLUTEN-FREE

GRAIN-FREE

KETO

VEGETARIAN

My mom makes spinach artichoke dip every Christmas and Easter, and since I can no longer eat mine out of a bread bowl, this triple-cheesy pizza removes the gluten from the equation and puts me back in the holiday spirit!

- 1 Cali'flour Pizza Crust (page 26)
- ½ cup (10 g) packed baby spinach
- ¼ cup (40 g) quartered artichoke hearts
- 4 tablespoons (30 g) shredded mozzarella cheese
- 1 tablespoon sour cream
- 1½ tablespoons cream cheese, softened
- 1 teaspoon mayonnaise
- ½ teaspoon red pepper flakes

Preheat the oven to 425°F (220°C). Line a baking sheet with parchment paper or get out your pizza pan and place your crust on it.

In a medium bowl, mix together the spinach, artichoke hearts, 2 tablespoons of the mozzarella, the sour cream, cream cheese, and mayonnaise until evenly coated. Spread the mixture over the pizza crust and top with the remaining 2 tablespoons mozzarella. Place in the oven and bake for 8 to 10 minutes, until the cheese is melted. Remove from the oven to a cutting board and garnish with the red pepper flakes. Slice and serve.

STAINLESS S

stir-fry-style pizza

SERVES 3

GLUTEN-FREE

GRAIN-FREE

KETO FRIENDLY

VEGETARIAN

In the early days of Cali'flour Foods, I would always have a stir-fry pizza on offer at the Chico Farmers' Market. Customers couldn't get enough of them. This take on my stir-fry calls for super-thin veggies that cook right into the pizza, so no actual stir-frying is required for this super-fast pizza. Feel free to swap in other veggies from your farmers' market or garden.

1 Cali'flour Pizza Crust (page 26)

2 tablespoons Roasted Garlic Cream (page 51; optional)

¼ cup (60 ml) Marinara Sauce (page 40)

¼ cup (30 g) shredded mozzarella cheese

¼ small zucchini, very thinly sliced into half-moons

1 small white mushroom, very thinly sliced

3 tablespoons very thinly sliced white onion

¼ cup (20 g) very small broccoli florets

Extra-virgin olive oil or coconut oil cooking spray

⅛ teaspoon flaky sea salt

Pinch of freshly ground black pepper

Dried garlic flakes (optional)

Preheat the oven to 425°F (220°C). Line a baking sheet with parchment paper or get out your pizza pan and put your crust on it.

Spread the garlic cream, if using, over the crust. Spread the marinara sauce on top, then add the cheese. Arrange the zucchini, mushroom, onion, and broccoli over the cheese. Spray with a light coating of cooking spray. Place in the oven and bake for 8 to 10 minutes, until everything is hot. Remove from the oven to a cutting board, then sprinkle on the salt and pepper and some garlic flakes, if using. Slice and serve.

meaty pizzas

If you've got someone at home who won't touch vegetables (I know you're out there!), this chapter is for you. I'm not one to promote concealing food groups. But if they don't ask and they still get to enjoy pepperoni, barbecue, and Hawaiian, why spoil a great pizza moment?

pepperoni pizza

SERVES 3

GLUTEN-FREE

GRAIN-FREE

KETO

You'll be amazed at the magic pepperoni, red sauce, and cheese make atop a Cali'flour crust. My boys would happily eat this pizza all day long, and it's a favorite of six-year-old Gavin, who, after a diagnosis of brain cancer, was put on a ketogenic diet limited to 10 net carbs a day. A serving contains few enough carbs that Gavin gets to enjoy pizza like any other little boy. Make sure the quality of your pepperoni matches that of your crust by choosing a brand that's all-natural, nitrate-free, and gluten-free.

- 1 Cali'flour Pizza Crust (page 26)
- ¼ cup (60 ml) Marinara Sauce (page 40)
- 1 ounce (28 g) pepperoni slices
- ¼ cup (30 g) grated mozzarella cheese
- 1 tablespoon torn fresh basil or parsley leaves
- Sprinkle of red pepper flakes (optional)

Preheat the oven to 425°F (220°C). Line a baking sheet with parchment paper or get out your pizza pan and put your crust on it.

Spread the sauce over the crust and arrange the pepperoni on top. Add the cheese, covering part of the pepperoni to keep it from curling as it bakes. Place in the oven and bake for 8 to 10 minutes, until the cheese is melted. Remove from the oven to a cutting board and add the basil and red pepper flakes, if using. Then slice and serve.

VARIATION

Turkey Pepperoni Pizza: *Swap in turkey pepperoni for pork pepperoni.*

meat lover's pizza

SERVES 3

GLUTEN-FREE

GRAIN-FREE

PALEO*

KETO FRIENDLY

DAIRY-FREE

* If skipping the wine in the bolognese sauce

So many people tell us their spouses who refuse to eat vegetables can't get enough of this one. If you're a dairy eater, you can finish yours with a sprinkle of mozzarella cheese.

- 1 Paleo Cali'flour Pizza Crust (page 29)
- ½ cup (120 ml) Quick Bolognese Sauce (page 42)
- 2 strips bacon, cooked and crumbled
- 1 ounce (28 g) cooked firm sausage, thinly sliced and seared in a hot pan
- Red pepper flakes (optional)
- Fresh oregano and/or parsley for garnish

Preheat the oven to 425°F (220°C). Line a baking sheet with parchment paper or get out your pizza pan and put your crust on it.

Spread the sauce over the crust and arrange the bacon and sausage on top. Sprinkle with red pepper flakes, if using. Place in the oven and bake for 8 to 10 minutes, until everything is hot. Remove from the oven to a serving plate, then slice and serve.

SWAP

To make this pizza keto friendly: Use a Cali'flour crust (page 26).

hawaiian pizza

SERVES 3

GLUTEN-FREE

GRAIN-FREE

KETO FRIENDLY

Salty plus sweet makes the Hawaiian my all-time favorite pizza, and 24 million Australians agree with me, as it's the most popular pizza in the Land Down Under. (Interestingly, the Hawaiian was invented by a Greek—Sam Panopoulos—who ran a pizza place in Canada!) To add a veggie element, throw in some thinly sliced peppers or mush-rooms, or to make it meatier, add pepperoni. A Spicy Jalapeño crust (page 26) would add a nice balance of heat.

- 1 Cali'flour Pizza Crust (page 26)
- ¼ cup (60 ml) Marinara Sauce (page 40)
- ¼ cup (40 g) cubed fresh pineapple (¼-inch/6-mm cubes)
- 1 ounce (28 g) thinly sliced ham, torn into pieces
- ¼ cup (30 g) shredded mozzarella cheese

Preheat the oven to 425°F (220°C). Line a baking sheet with parchment paper or get out your pizza pan and put your crust on it.

Spread the marinara sauce over the crust. Arrange the pineapple and ham over the sauce and top with the cheese. Place in the oven and bake for 8 to 10 minutes, until the cheese is melted. Remove from the oven to a cutting board, add pepper flakes, if using, then slice and serve.

DURALEX

tandoori-style chicken pizza

SERVES 3, WITH EXTRA TANDOORI-STYLE CHICKEN

GLUTEN-FREE

GRAIN-FREE

KETO FRIENDLY

The secret to a tender chicken tandoori is marinating the chicken in yogurt for three to four hours before cooking it in a clay oven called a *tandoor*. But most of us don't have room for a second oven at home, so Chef Nash Patel, of the Dosa Kitchen food truck in Vermont, has shared with us his simple, equally delicious home kitchen version. It won't be bright red like the tandoori chicken we see at Indian restaurants, because it gets its color from cayenne, paprika, and turmeric rather than artificial red dye. You'll only need a quarter of the chicken for your pizza—you can make additional pizzas, or enjoy the rest over Cauliflower Rice (page 36).

You can find the spices for this recipe in most supermarkets, Indian grocers, or online.

TANDOORI-STYLE CHICKEN

- 12 ounces (340 g) boneless, skinless dark meat chicken, cut into ½-inch (12-mm) pieces
- ¼ cup (60 ml) whole milk Greek yogurt
- 1 teaspoon minced fresh ginger
- 1 clove garlic, minced
- 1 tablespoon ground coriander
- 1 teaspoon ground cumin
- ½ teaspoon cayenne pepper
- ½ teaspoon paprika
- ½ teaspoon ground turmeric
- ¼ teaspoon garam masala
- ¾ teaspoon sea salt
- 1 tablespoon ghee

PIZZA

- 1 Cali'flour Pizza Crust (page 26)
- ¼ cup (60 ml) Marinara Sauce (page 40)
- ¼ cup (30 g) shredded mozzarella cheese
- Sliced green chiles (optional)

MAKE THE TANDOORI-STYLE CHICKEN: Put the chicken in a medium container. Spoon the yogurt into a small bowl and whisk in the ginger, garlic, coriander, cumin, cayenne, paprika, turmeric, garam masala, and salt. Add the spiced yogurt to the chicken and stir to coat. Cover and place in the refrigerator to marinate for 3 to 4 hours.

Preheat the oven to 425°F (220°C). Line a baking sheet with parchment paper.

Place the chicken on the baking sheet in a single layer, removing any excess marinade. Place in the oven and roast for 15 minutes, then brush with the ghee and roast for another 10 minutes, or until browned on top. Remove from the oven and leave the oven on.

MAKE THE PIZZA: Line another baking sheet with parchment paper or get out your pizza pan and put your crust on it.

Spread the marinara sauce over the crust. Arrange ½ cup (100 g) chicken over the sauce and top with the cheese and chiles, if using. Place in the oven and bake for 8 to 10 minutes, until the cheese is melted. Remove from the oven to a cutting board, then slice and serve.

antipasto pizza with dijon mayo

SERVES 3

GLUTEN-FREE

GRAIN-FREE

KETO

With just a few ingredients, this pizza comes together in minutes yet makes a powerful presentation. A mustard-mayo base gives a creamy, tangy counterpoint to the umami-rich toppings. Feel free to mix and match with any antipasto ingredients that call to you, such as salami, fresh mozzarella, pepperoncini, or marinated artichoke hearts. I recommend using an Italian Seasoning crust (page 26) for this one.

2 tablespoons Dijon mustard

2 tablespoons mayonnaise

1 Cali'flour Pizza Crust (page 26), baked for a few minutes longer than specified in the recipe

1 ounce (28 g/2 slices) thinly sliced prosciutto, torn into small pieces

1 ounce (28 g) shaved pecorino cheese

5 fresh figs, cut in half (optional)

1 heaping tablespoon sliced mixed pitted olives (optional)

4 large fresh basil leaves, torn

In a small bowl, whisk the mustard with the mayonnaise. Spread the mustard mayo over the crust and add the toppings. Slice and serve.

fennel, onion, and pepper bolognese pizza

SERVES 3

GLUTEN-FREE

GRAIN-FREE

PALEO*

KETO FRIENDLY

DAIRY-FREE

* If skipping the wine in the bolognese sauce

Fennel is great for digestion, is known to decrease inflammation, and adds a sweet, anise-like flavor to this meaty pizza. To make the pizza meatier, go ahead and crumble some crispy bacon on top.

- 1 Paleo Cali'flour Pizza Crust (page 29)
- ½ cup (120 ml) Quick Bolognese Sauce (page 42)
- ¼ cup (25 g) very thinly sliced orange, red, or yellow bell pepper
- ¼ cup (20 g) very thinly sliced fennel, fronds reserved
- 2 tablespoons very thinly sliced onion
- Extra-virgin olive oil cooking spray
- 2 teaspoons Plant-Based Parmesan Cheese (page 55)

Preheat the oven to 425°F (220°C). Line a baking sheet with parchment paper or get out your pizza pan and put your crust on it.

Spread the sauce over the crust. Arrange the bell pepper, fennel, and onion over the crust. Give the vegetables a light coating of cooking spray. Place in the oven and bake for 8 to 10 minutes, until everything is hot. Remove from the oven to a cutting board, top with the cheese, then slice and serve.

cheeseburger pizza

SERVES 3

GLUTEN-FREE

GRAIN-FREE

KETO FRIENDLY

Pickles on pizza? You betcha! If you're a burger lover, you probably already have all the ingredients in the house—just take the bun out of the equation. For the healthiest results, use sugar-free ketchup and mustard and naturally fermented pickles, and to finish your pizza with dramatic flair, apply your mayo with a squeeze bottle. This recipe is inspired by one Guy Fieri came across on his travels via his show *Diners, Drive-Ins and Dives*.

TIP

Prebake the crust for a couple of extra minutes to crisp it up sufficiently to hold the juicy toppings.

- 1 Cali'flour Pizza Crust (page 26)
- 4 ounces (115 g) ground beef
- ⅛ teaspoon sea salt
- 2 tablespoons ketchup
- 1 tablespoon mustard
- ¼ cup (30 g) shredded Cheddar cheese
- ½ small dill pickle, sliced
- 2 tablespoons slivered red onion
- 1 tablespoon mayonnaise
- ¼ cup (15 g) shredded romaine lettuce

Preheat the oven to 425°F (220°C). Line a baking sheet with parchment paper or get out your pizza pan and put your crust on it.

Cook the beef in a medium skillet over medium-high heat, stirring to break it up, for about 7 minutes, until no longer pink. Drain any excess fat, stir in the salt, and let cool slightly.

In a small bowl, whisk the ketchup and mustard.

Spread the ketchup mixture over the crust. Arrange the beef on top and scatter the cheese over the beef. Place in the oven and bake for 8 to 10 minutes, until the cheese is melted. Remove from the oven to a cutting board and top with the pickle and red onion. Drizzle the mayonnaise on top and finish with the lettuce. Slice and serve.

barbecue pork pizza

SERVES 3

GLUTEN-FREE

GRAIN-FREE

PALEO

DAIRY-FREE

Because I love salty and sweet so much, I'm crazy for this barbecue pork pizza. It comes complete with a refreshing fennel slaw that you can make while the pizza is in the oven. Add the slaw just before serving. There will be plenty of barbecue sauce left over for additional pizzas or to freeze for future pies.

PIZZA

1 Cali'flour Pizza Crust (page 26)

¼ cup (60 ml) plus 1 tablespoon Barbecue Sauce (recipe follows)

½ cup (100 g) shredded cooked pork

FENNEL SLAW

¼ cup (20 g) very thinly sliced fennel

1 tablespoon grated carrot

2 teaspoons mayonnaise

1 teaspoon finely chopped fresh flat-leaf parsley

⅛ teaspoon sea salt

2 teaspoons minced fresh flat-leaf parsley

MAKE THE PIZZA: Preheat the oven to 425°F (220°C). Line a baking sheet with parchment paper or get out your pizza pan and put your crust on it.

Spread ¼ cup (60 ml) of the barbecue sauce over the crust. In a small bowl, toss the pork with the remaining 1 tablespoon barbecue sauce to coat. Arrange the pork over the crust. Place in the oven and bake for 8 to 10 minutes, until everything is hot.

While the pizza is in the oven, MAKE THE FENNEL SLAW: In a small bowl, combine the fennel and carrot. Add the mayonnaise and toss to coat. Stir in the parsley and salt.

Remove the pizza from the oven to a cutting board and top with the slaw, garnish with the parsley, then slice and serve.

barbecue sauce

MAKES ABOUT 1½ CUPS (360 ML)

2 tablespoons extra-virgin olive oil

2 cloves garlic, minced

1 teaspoon chili powder

1 cup (240 ml) ketchup

3 tablespoons molasses

2 tablespoons coconut sugar

2 tablespoons apple cider vinegar

2 tablespoons Worcestershire sauce

2 tablespoons Dijon mustard

1 tablespoon hot sauce

Heat the oil in a medium saucepan over medium heat. Add the garlic and cook for 30 seconds. Add the chili powder and cook for another 30 seconds. Add the ketchup, molasses, coconut sugar, vinegar, Worcestershire sauce, mustard, and hot sauce. Bring to a simmer, then reduce the heat to medium-low and simmer, uncovered, for about 20 minutes, until thickened. Cool completely before using. The sauce will keep, covered and refrigerated, for up to 1 week.

thai-inspired pork pizza

SERVES 3

GLUTEN-FREE

GRAIN-FREE

KETO FRIENDLY

I learned to love the flavors of Thai food in my thirties. Paleo guru Robb Wolfe and his wife, Nicki Violetti, owned a CrossFit gym in Chico, where I'm from. Robb suggested we try his favorite Thai restaurant in town that had a paleo-friendly menu, and I was hooked! A toss in lime juice and fish sauce gives the pork its characteristic Thai flavor, and a generous sprinkle of herbs adds a refreshing finish. You can find chili garlic sauce in Asian food stores and some supermarkets. If unavailable, try sriracha. You may substitute another meat such as chicken, beef, or turkey if you like.

- 1 Cali'flour Pizza Crust (page 26)
- 1½ tablespoons chili garlic sauce
- ½ cup (100 g) shredded cooked pork
- 1 teaspoon fresh lime juice
- 1 teaspoon fish sauce
- ¼ cup (30 g) shredded mozzarella cheese
- 2 tablespoons red onion slivers
- ¼ cup (8 g) loosely packed mixed small fresh Thai basil and mint leaves (tear larger leaves)

Preheat the oven to 425°F (220°C). Line a baking sheet with parchment paper or get out your pizza pan and put your crust on it.

Spread the chili garlic sauce over the crust. In a small bowl, toss the pork with the lime juice and fish sauce. Add the cheese and toss to combine, then spread the mixture evenly over the crust. Place in the oven and bake for 8 to 10 minutes, until the cheese is melted. Remove from the oven to a cutting board, then top with the onion and herbs. Slice and serve.

asparagus, prosciutto, and parmesan pizza

SERVES 3

GLUTEN-FREE

GRAIN-FREE

KETO FRIENDLY

I love grilling asparagus, but for the convenience of a weeknight pizza, I bypass the barbecue and shave the asparagus with a vegetable peeler so it cooks right into the cheese as it melts deliciously into the crust.

- 1 Cali'flour Pizza Crust (page 26)
- 1 tablespoon grainy mustard
- 4 stalks asparagus, ends trimmed
- ½ teaspoon extra-virgin olive oil
- Pinch of sea salt
- ¼ cup (25 g) shredded Fontina cheese
- 2 tablespoons ricotta cheese
- 1 tablespoon finely grated Parmesan cheese
- 1 ounce (28 g/2 slices) prosciutto, torn into large pieces
- Coarsely ground black pepper

Preheat the oven to 425°F (220°C). Line a baking sheet with parchment paper or get out your pizza pan and put your crust on it.

Spread the mustard over the crust. Shave the asparagus using a vegetable peeler. Place the asparagus in a medium bowl, drizzle the oil over the asparagus, and add the salt. Toss to coat. Add the Fontina, ricotta, and Parmesan and toss to combine. Spread the mixture evenly over the crust and top with the prosciutto.

Place in the oven and bake for 8 to 10 minutes, until the cheese is melted. Remove from the oven to a cutting board, sprinkle with pepper, then slice and serve.

SWAP

To make this pizza vegetarian: Omit the prosciutto and increase the asparagus to 6 stalks.

seafood pizzas

This chapter is inspired by one of my favorite places on earth, San Francisco's Fisherman's Wharf. The Wharf has had a special spot in my heart ever since my family and I ran the Bay to Breakers dressed as Velveeta cheese, inspired by an old Herb Caen article in the *San Francisco Chronicle* (which is also the first time I saw naked people running a race, but I digress). The recipes include a pizza based on my favorite cream cheese and lox bagel and pizzas containing shrimp, crab, and clams.

dilly cream cheese and lox pizza

SERVES 3

GLUTEN-FREE

GRAIN-FREE

KETO FRIENDLY

Cream cheese and lox on a bagel was particularly hard to give up for me, but like an old friend, cauliflower came to the rescue once again in the form of this pizza. You could also build your cream cheese and lox on a bagel using the recipe on page 62.

- ¼ cup (55 g) cream cheese, softened
- 1 Cali'flour Pizza Crust (page 26), baked for a few minutes longer than specified in the recipe
- 2 ounces (55 g) lox slices
- 2 teaspoons chopped fresh dill
- 2 teaspoons capers (optional)
- Squeeze of fresh lemon juice, plus lemon slices for serving

Spread the cream cheese over the crust. Top with the lox, scatter the dill and capers on top, and finish with the lemon juice. Slice and serve.

SWAP

To make this pizza paleo: Swap a Paleo crust (page 29) for the Cali'flour crust and use Cashew Cream Cheese (page 59) or a store-bought creamy nut cheese instead of dairy cream cheese.

green salsa shrimp pizza

SERVES 3

GLUTEN-FREE

GRAIN-FREE

PALEO

KETO FRIENDLY

DAIRY-FREE

Fresh, slightly tangy green salsa blankets sweet, garlicky shrimp in this south of the border–style pizza. If you don't have small shrimp, you can cut large shrimp in half lengthwise. Chop the bell pepper very fine so you can sprinkle it over like confetti.

2 teaspoons extra-virgin olive oil

4 ounces (115 g) small shrimp, peeled and deveined

2 pinches of sea salt

⅔ cup (165 ml) Green Salsa (page 46)

1 Paleo Cali'flour Pizza Crust (page 29), baked for a few minutes longer than specified in the recipe

2 tablespoons Almond Ricotta (page 58; optional)

2 tablespoons finely chopped yellow, orange, or red bell pepper

1 tablespoon torn fresh cilantro leaves

Heat the oil in a medium skillet over medium-high heat. Sprinkle the shrimp with a pinch of salt and add them to the pan one by one in clockwise order around the edge of the pan without touching and cook without stirring until the shrimp start to turn pink, 1 to 2 minutes. Using tongs, turn the shrimp in the order you placed them in the pan and cook until the second side turns pink and the shrimp are just about cooked through, another 1 to 2 minutes. Add the salsa and cook just to heat through. Spread the salsa and shrimp over the crust, top with dollops of the ricotta, if using, the bell pepper, and cilantro. Slice and serve.

clam and bacon pizza

SERVES 3

GLUTEN-FREE

GRAIN-FREE

KETO FRIENDLY

Clams are one of the most sustainable forms of seafood in the United States. This pizza makes the most of their briny flavor by pairing them with fatty, salty bacon, serving them over a red sauce, and adding a cheesy finish.

- 1 Cali'flour Pizza Crust (page 26)
- ¼ cup (60 ml) plus 1 tablespoon Marinara Sauce (page 40)
- 1 (6½-ounce/185-g) can clams, drained, or ½ cup (50 g) chopped fresh clams
- 1 strip bacon, cooked and crumbled
- ¼ cup (30 g) shredded mozzarella cheese
- 2 teaspoons chopped fresh parsley

Preheat the oven to 425°F (220°C). Line a baking sheet with parchment paper or get out your pizza pan and put your crust on it.

Spread ¼ cup (60 ml) of the marinara sauce over the crust. Put the clams in a small bowl and toss with the remaining 1 tablespoon sauce. Arrange the clams over the crust, scatter the bacon over the crust, and top with the cheese. Place in the oven and bake for 8 to 10 minutes, until the cheese is melted. Remove from the oven to a cutting board, sprinkle with the parsley, then slice and serve.

VARIATION

Clams in White Sauce Pizza: *Substitute White Sauce (page 44) for the Marinara Sauce.*

crab alfredo pizza

SERVES 3

GLUTEN-FREE

GRAIN-FREE

PALEO

KETO FRIENDLY

DAIRY-FREE

White sauce made from cauliflower, cashews, and coconut transformed my conception of alfredo, and with a little help from plant-based Parmesan, it's now possible to enjoy this dish dairy-free.

1 Paleo Cali'flour Pizza Crust (page 29)

6 tablespoons (90 ml) White Sauce (page 44)

½ cup (2 ounces/55 g) crab meat, drained and patted with a paper towel

3 cherry tomatoes, thinly sliced

1 tablespoon finely chopped scallion

2 teaspoons Plant-Based Parmesan Cheese (page 55)

1 teaspoon capers, plus a little caper juice

1½ teaspoons finely chopped fresh tarragon (optional)

Preheat the oven to 425°F (220°C). Line a baking sheet with parchment paper or get out your pizza pan and put your crust on it.

Spread 3 tablespoons of the white sauce over the crust. Place the crab in a small bowl and toss with the remaining 3 tablespoons sauce. Spread the crab over the crust and top with the tomatoes and scallion.

Place in the oven and bake for 8 to 10 minutes, until everything is hot. Remove from the oven to a cutting board and top with the cheese, capers, caper juice, and tarragon, if using. Slice and serve.

sweet treats

Cauliflower's ability to transform into something sweet is one of the crucifer's greatest magic tricks. Whether it's chocolate and cheese on a pizza, apple with a slice of cheddar, or the moistest gluten-free cookies you could ever wish for, this sweetaholic promises that cauliflower won't disappoint in the dessert department!

strawberry honey pie

SERVES 4

GLUTEN-FREE

GRAIN-FREE

KETO FRIENDLY

VEGETARIAN

Stephanie Galland, of the Cali'flour team, and I have served versions of this strawberry pie at the ESPY and Emmy pre-parties. Watching large professional athletes gobble up this plant-based masterpiece made my heart sing. The legendary Tony Hawk adored it. And we even got Wanda Durant, Kevin Durant's veggie-fearing mom, to innocently enjoy a slice. She flipped out when she was told that she had just eaten a vegetable and loved it! It is only natural that Stephanie, a beautiful friend inside and out, would create such a sweet honey of a pie. Make sure to use a plain crust for this one and consider finishing with a drizzle of balsamic vinegar for a flavor contrast.

¼ cup (55 g) Cashew Cream Cheese (page 59), at room temperature

1 Plant-Based Cali'flour Pizza Crust (page 28), baked for a few minutes longer than specified in the recipe

⅓ cup (55 g) sliced fresh strawberries

2 teaspoons slivered almonds

2 teaspoons runny honey

Spread the cream cheese over the crust. Arrange the strawberries and slivered almonds over the crust and drizzle the honey over the top. Slice and serve.

caramel apple pie

SERVES 4, WITH EXTRA APPLE FILLING

GLUTEN-FREE

GRAIN-FREE

KETO FRIENDLY

VEGETARIAN

My daughter, Caroline, is an old soul and loves to make masterpieces with her food. She will often make apple pie, and as a mom, of course I don't want to disappoint her by not eating her creations. With this version, I can now eat apple pie without worrying about it bringing on inflammation.

Cheese and apple are a classic pie combination, so starting with a basic Cali'flour Pizza Crust was a natural. Make sure to use a plain crust for this recipe and, to take the cheese pairing a step further, serve with a slice of Cheddar alongside, as in the variation below. The apple filling makes enough for two pizzas; reheat leftover filling before using it.

- 1 tablespoon ghee or unsalted butter
- 1 teaspoon ground cinnamon, plus more for sprinkling
- ⅛ teaspoon grated nutmeg
- 2 cups (320 g) peeled and chopped apples (3 medium apples)
- ¼ cup (35 g) coconut sugar
- ⅛ teaspoon sea salt
- 1 tablespoon tapioca flour
- 1¼ teaspoons fresh lemon juice
- 1 Cali'flour Pizza Crust (page 26), baked for a few minutes longer than specified in the recipe

In a small saucepan, melt the ghee over medium-low heat. Add the cinnamon and nutmeg and stir until fragrant, about 30 seconds. Add the apples, coconut sugar, salt, and 3 tablespoons water and stir well to coat the apple pieces. Increase the heat to medium, cover, and cook, stirring a few times, for 5 minutes, or until the apples have softened.

Meanwhile, whisk the tapioca and 1 tablespoon water together in a very small bowl. Drizzle into the apple filling, stir to combine, and cook for another 3 to 5 minutes, until the apple mixture is dark in color, thick, and gooey. Remove from the heat and stir in the lemon juice. Spread half of the apple filling over the pizza crust, sprinkle with cinnamon, and serve.

VARIATION

Cheddar Apple Pie: *Accompany your pizza with a slice of Cheddar cheese.*

chile chocolate pie

SERVES 4

GLUTEN-FREE

GRAIN-FREE

KETO FRIENDLY

VEGETARIAN

Inspired by our Spicy Jalapeño crust and the classic chocolate and chile pairing, this dessert pizza is simply to die for. Tangy goat cheese and fresh mint give a cooling contrast. Orange-flavored dark chocolate works particularly well in this recipe.

3 ounces (85 g) dark chocolate, chopped

Pinch of cayenne pepper

2 ounces (55 g) soft goat cheese, at room temperature

2 tablespoons heavy cream

1 Spicy Jalapeño Cali'flour Pizza Crust (page 26), baked for a few minutes longer than specified in the recipe

1 tablespoon slivered almonds

Small fresh mint leaves

Put the chocolate in a small heatproof bowl. Bring about 1 inch (2.5 cm) of water to a simmer in a small saucepan. Set the bowl atop the pot, making sure the water doesn't touch the bottom of the bowl. Stir the chocolate frequently until almost completely melted, then remove from the heat and stir until fully melted. Add the cayenne. Let cool.

Put the goat cheese in a small bowl. Add the cream and whisk with a fork to incorporate. Spread the goat cheese mixture over the crust. Drizzle the chocolate over the crust in any design you like, then top with the almonds and mint. Slice and serve.

pear and honey tartlets

MAKES 6

GLUTEN-FREE

GRAIN-FREE

KETO FRIENDLY

VEGETARIAN

These no-cook little tarts highlight ripe seasonal pears with a drizzle of honey to bring out their natural sweetness. Thick, dark buckwheat honey adds a strong molasses flavor that stands out against creamy mascarpone, but you can use any pourable honey. Make sure to use a plain crust for this recipe, and save the scraps left from cutting out the crust circles to make breadcrumbs (page 35).

- 1 Cali'flour Pizza Crust (page 26)
- 3 tablespoons mascarpone cheese or crème fraîche, at room temperature
- 1 small ripe pear, cored and cut into slices to fit the crust circles
- 1 tablespoon runny honey, preferably buckwheat honey
- Ground cardamom

Preheat the oven to 425°F (220°C) and line a baking sheet with parchment paper.

Use a 2½- to 3-inch (6- to 7.5-cm) cookie cutter or the top of a drinking glass to cut out 6 rounds of crust. Place on the prepared baking sheet and bake, turning once, until they are crispy and well browned, 7 to 10 minutes. Remove from the oven and cool.

Spread 1½ teaspoons of the mascarpone over each crust. Top with pieces of pear and drizzle the honey on top. Finish with a sprinkle of cardamom.

nana's chocolate chip cookies

MAKES ABOUT 42

GLUTEN-FREE

GRAIN-FREE

KETO FRIENDLY

VEGETARIAN

My mother-in-law, Diana Lacey, was born in New Zealand to a truly health-conscious family. She brought her clean-eating ways with her to the United States, and now at the age of seventy-five you'd think she was fifty. This tribute to Diana fortifies her already gluten-free chocolate chip cookie recipe with cauliflower meal for a pillowy soft treat. When Nana comes to visit, you can bet she will bring her chocolate chip cookies and her perfect pavlova!

This is a great recipe to make with kids because they get to use their hands to form the cookies. Note: These cookies are done when they're browned on the bottom—they don't need to brown on top, and will be soft when you take them out. They firm up as they cool.

- ¼ cup (½ stick/55 g) unsalted butter, softened
- ½ cup (70 g) coconut sugar
- 2 large eggs
- 1 cup (240 ml) unsweetened applesauce
- ½ cup (120 ml) smooth unsweetened almond butter
- 1 cup (110 g) coconut flour
- ¼ cup (35 g) ground flax seeds
- 1 tablespoon baking soda
- ½ teaspoon sea salt
- 5 ounces (140 g/1 cup loosely crumbled) Cauliflower Meal (page 20)
- 1 cup (175 g) stevia-sweetened chocolate chips, such as Lily's

Preheat the oven to 375°F (190°C) and line two baking sheets with parchment paper.

In a large bowl, use a wooden spoon or rubber spatula to mix the butter and coconut sugar until combined and creamy and it comes together as a loose ball. Add one egg at a time and mix until fully incorporated. Add the applesauce and mix until incorporated. Add the almond butter and mix until incorporated.

In a medium bowl, combine the coconut flour, flax seeds, baking soda, and salt. Add the cauliflower meal and use your fingers to fully mix it into the dry ingredients. Add the cauliflower meal mixture to the wet ingredients and stir in the chocolate chips. Let the dough rest for 10 minutes.

Measure out tablespoons of dough and roll them around in your hands. Place on the baking sheets and press until ½ inch (12 mm) thick, then make crisscross indentations with the tines of a fork. Bake for 12 to 14 minutes, until lightly browned on the bottom. Let cool completely on the sheets. The cookies will keep in a covered container in the refrigerator for up to 5 days, or in the freezer for up to 1 month. Bring to room temperature before serving.

VARIATIONS

Cherry Orange: *Add 1 tablespoon grated orange zest to the wet ingredients and 1 cup (145 g) dried cherries when you add the chocolate chips.*

Cinnamon Walnut: *Add 1 tablespoon ground cinnamon to the dry ingredients and 1 cup (120 g) chopped walnuts when you add the chocolate chips.*

coconut macaroons

MAKES ABOUT 20 COOKIES

GLUTEN-FREE
GRAIN-FREE
PALEO
KETO FRIENDLY

VEGETARIAN
DAIRY-FREE

My daughter, Caroline, and I came up with this recipe when Cali'flour Foods was just a spark of a dream, but I knew one day it would be a recipe we'd share with the world!

- 3 large egg whites
- ¼ teaspoon cream of tartar
- ¼ teaspoon sea salt
- ½ cup (70 g) coconut sugar
- 1 teaspoon pure vanilla extract
- 2½ ounces (70 g/½ cup loosely crumbled) Cauliflower Meal (page 20)
- 1½ cups (120 g) shredded unsweetened coconut
- 2 teaspoons orange zest
- ¼ cup (45 g) stevia-sweetened chocolate chips, such as Lily's, or cacao nibs (optional)

Preheat the oven to 325°F (165°C) and line a baking sheet with parchment paper.

In a large bowl using a handheld mixer, beat the egg whites with the cream of tartar and salt until soft peaks form. Add the coconut sugar and vanilla and beat until combined.

In a separate bowl, combine the cauliflower meal, coconut, and orange zest and mix with your fingers to combine and smooth out any lumps of cauliflower meal. Fold the cauliflower meal mixture into the egg whites one third at a time. Allow to rest for 10 minutes. Fold in the chocolate chips, if using.

Scoop out 1 tablespoon dough and roll it in your hands to form a ball, then place on the prepared baking sheet. Repeat with the remaining dough. If you wish, make triangle shapes using your fingertips to peak the dough, or flatten the dough into discs. Place on the baking sheet and bake for 20 minutes, or until lightly colored on the bottom with some specks of color on top. Cool completely on the sheet. The cookies will keep, refrigerated, for up to 5 days or frozen for up to 1 month. Bring to room temperature before serving.

VARIATION

Cocoa Coconut Macaroons: *Replace the vanilla with ½ teaspoon almond extract and add 2 tablespoons unsweetened cocoa powder as you add the coconut sugar.*

dietary notes

The following is a key to the dietary markers you'll find with each recipe.

Gluten-Free

Gluten is not used in any form in any of our pizza crusts or in any of the recipes in this book. Autoimmune diseases can be controlled by an anti-inflammatory diet, and gluten is on my list of inflammatory foods that I gave up after being diagnosed with lupus. Foods that decrease inflammation are vegetables high in antioxidants, which includes cauliflower. So a gluten-free cauliflower pizza crust means people like me and those of us who are gluten-sensitive, allergic, or suffering from celiac disease can enjoy pizza again!

Grain-Free

For many people, grains as well as gluten can cause inflammation. There is a little-known factor in food that is commonly referred to as cross reactivity/sensitivity. That's a fancy way to say that the proteins in some nonwheat foods instigate a similar response to wheat in people sensitive to gluten. Even those who are fine with gluten can have a reaction to grains because of their inflammatory nature. For this reason, paleo, keto, and low-carb diets go grain-free and focus instead on vegetable starches for their carbs. This means no significant spikes in blood sugar without sacrificing that necessary fiber. All of our crusts and all of the recipes in this book are grain-free.

Paleo

Because our basic pizza crust contains cheese, it is not paleo, as a paleo diet is not only gluten-free and grain-free but dairy-free as well. Dairy can contribute to inflammation when eaten in large amounts, so our Paleo pizza crusts can be considered fully anti-inflammatory. Paleo essentially forces you to eat more vegetables in order to keep satiated, which is never a bad thing! The Paleo pizza crusts are perfect for the protein-minded, and they're so full of flavor you won't notice the lack of cheese. The Paleo crust, which includes eggs, partners with a vegetarian diet but not a vegan diet.

Keto

Not too long ago, fat-free diets were all the rage. Expanding waistlines and an increase in chronic disease were the unintended results of this misguided trend. It turns out our bodies and brains need healthy fats to function. And by omitting fat from our diets we started overeating carbs and sugar because we found we could munch on them endlessly without filling up. To fix this fattening epidemic, many of us are turning to ketogenic diets. Ketosis is a state of fat loss brought on by following a diet very low in net carbs, no more than 20 grams a day, with moderate protein, and high in (good) fat. When there are no carbs to burn for fuel, your body begins to burn fat instead. The breakdown product of fat is called ketones, and the body goes into a state of ketosis. Ketosis is literally the burning of your stored fat for energy. A basic Cali'flour Pizza Crust is a keto eater's answer to comfort food, as it is super low in carbs and nourishes your body with lots of veggie goodness. It's just the thing to help kick carb cravings and get rid of those unwanted pounds!

You'll see indicators for both "keto" and "keto friendly" on our recipes. The difference between the two is simple, but does require a bit of explanation. Because the keto diet relies on *daily* intake, I've broken it down into "keto," meals whose serving size fits the exact definition of keto, which is high-fat, moderate protein, and low- to no-carb; and "keto friendly," meals that complement a keto diet because they are low- or no-carb but not necessarily high-fat.

Low-carb vs. keto

A general low-carb diet is more flexible than keto in that you simply eat fewer carbs than everything else. Typically a person on a low-carb diet will eat high-protein, moderate fat, and low-carb. The carb intake may still be pretty significant, but as long as it's noticeably less than the fat and protein intake, it's commonly referred to as low-carb. The benefits of a low-carb diet include lasting weight and fat loss, cognitive improvement, fewer cravings, decreased inflammation, and lower risk for type 2 diabetes and heart disease. All that, and you get to eat pizza! In comparison, the goal of a ketogenic diet is to put your body in ketosis by eating no more than 20 grams of total carbs per day with moderate protein. Note: Our crusts are low-glycemic, too (the glycemic index is a tool used to indicate how a food affects blood sugar levels).

Vegan (Plant-Based)

The Plant-Based pizza crust, based on cauliflower and seeds, is for vegans and people who don't or can't eat eggs or nuts. Dairy can contribute to inflammation when eaten in large amounts, so our Plant-Based pizza crusts can be considered fully anti-inflammatory. One of our goals when developing this crust was to create a crust that people with just about any kind of allergies could still enjoy. No nuts, no dairy, *and* it fits into the other major diet categories described above.

acknowledgments

In recognition of my wonderful coauthor, Leda Scheintaub: This book is as much your labor of love as it is mine. You have been an incredible guide on this journey and an absolute joy to work with. I'm so grateful for your help in bringing my words to life.

A huge thanks to the team at Abrams Books. Holly Dolce, you have cheered us on since day one. Your wisdom is beyond words. I feel so blessed to have you as a mentor. Your support and how welcomed I was by the entire Abrams staff have meant the world to me. In particular, art director Deb Wood and Liam Flanagan in the design department helped make this book look its very best. Publicist Jen Bastien and Kim Sheu in the marketing department promoted the book with enthusiasm. Managing editor Lisa Silverman skillfully ushered the book through the production process. Liana Krissoff both copyedited the book and tested several crucial recipes. Additional creative support in the kitchen came from Lizi Rosenberg and Katie Eyles.

To my agents from Sterling Lord, Jaidree Braddix, Celeste Fine, and Sarah Passick: Thank you for taking a chance on me. You believed in me when I doubted myself. This book is real because of you.

Heartfelt thanks to my two talented photography teams, Andrew Purcell and Carrie Purcell in California, and Clare Barboza and Gretchen Rude in Vermont. You made this cookbook look far better than I could have hoped!

Immense love to my parents, who are the reason Cali'flour Foods has come this far. Mom and Ken, "thank you" is not enough for what you have done for me. From packaging orders in the early days to refinancing your house to help fund the mass production of our pizza crusts, your belief in me has been the solid foundation on which I've built my dreams. Mom, I still remember when you were a book buyer for our local college and took me to my first ABA book convention in 1984. You introduced me to my love of books, and I hope this one will make you proud.

Endless gratitude to Jimi Sturgeon-Smith, my COO and right-hand woman. Your feedback and friendship mean more to me than you will ever know. You have shown unconditional loyalty to me and Cali'flour Foods. I could not have asked for a better partner in this endeavor.

To Doug Smith, Cali'flour's chief research and development guru. Your nutrition expertise has been instrumental in bringing this book to fruition and to the continued growth of our company. Thank you for the late nights, early mornings, and sacrifices you have made to support this company. I admire your knowledge and wisdom.

Much appreciation to my business coach, Chris Winfield. Thank you for introducing me to my book agents and setting in motion the fulfillment of my dream to create a cookbook.

A standing ovation for my wonderful team at Cali'flour Foods. You are my chosen family, and it is my greatest honor to work with such passionate, caring individuals. Words fail to express my gratitude for each and every one of you. None of this would be possible without your hard work and dedication to changing lives through serving our customers.

A special shout-out to my sassy, beautiful "sisters" I never had, Nicole Mimbs and Stephanie Galland. How I got so lucky to work with my best friends, I will never know. You have been there for me since the beginning and did the grunt work, from packing boxes in a hot warehouse to cleaning bathrooms, without complaint. Cheers to fifteen years of friendship and many more memories together with our families. I can't wait to celebrate with you at the end of this adventure.

Also to Ellen Yin, for capturing my voice. You are so wise and graceful at such a young age. Thank you for helping me think outside the box.

Last, and most important, a love note to our fans and customers. Thanks to you, our loyal Cali'fam, for being brave enough to try cauliflower pizza crusts with us before they were cool. For bringing us into your homes and family pizza nights. For sharing us with friends, sneaking our crusts to your kids, and raving about us to anyone who will listen. You all are pioneers, and together we will continue to revolutionize healthy eating so that food *always* tastes as good as it makes you feel. From the bottom of my heart, thank you, thank you, thank you. This is for you.

recipe index

Dairy-Free

Gluten-Free & Grain-Free

Keto

Keto Friendly

Paleo

Vegan

Vegetarian

index